FAMOUS VICTORY

The Gulf War

Patrick Bishop

'And everybody praised the Duke
Who this great fight did win.'
'But what good came of it at last?'
Quoth little Peterkin.
'Why that I cannot tell said he,
'But 'twas a famous victory.'
Robert Southey
After Blenheim

SINCLAIR-STEVENSON

Also by Patrick Bishop

The Winter War
(with John Witherow)
The Provisional I.R.A.
(with Eamonn Mallie)

First published in Great Britain by
Sinclair-Stevenson Limited
7/8 Kendrick Mews
London SW7 3HG England

British Library Cataloguing in Publication Data
A CIP catalogue record for this book is available from the British Library.

ISBN: 1 85619 140 0

Typeset by Rowland Phototypesetting Limited
Bury St Edmunds, Suffolk
Printed and bound in Great Britain by
Clays Limited, St Ives plc

FOR
MARIE

INTRODUCTION

On Sunday 29 July 1990 I checked out of the Sheraton Hotel in Kuwait City with a light heart, reasonably confident that the crisis between Kuwait and its bullying neighbour, Iraq, would be resolved without violence.

It was seven months later when I saw the Sheraton again. In the meantime it had undergone a dramatic change for the worse. The walls were black with smoke from the fires set by the Iraqi troops just before they'd pulled out. The greenery that used to mask and soften the harsh concrete angles of the entrance had sprouted, untamed. Through the padlocked door of the foyer the marble floor was carpeted in shards of glass. For a moment one felt like a South American explorer stumbling on a forgotten city which had been overwhelmed by the primeval force of the jungle.

The image fitted the general metaphor employed by America and the allies to explain what had happened. Here was Kuwait: small, rich, sophisticated, a point of light in a dark region. Next door: the barbarians and the barbarian leader who lived by the rule of the jungle.

The destruction wrought by the invaders certainly had a manic, gleeful edge. Driving across the desert with the Kuwaiti army, we had seen the black columns coiling up from the well-heads – blotting out the sun and speckling everything in blobs of oil. It was a historic act of pure vandalism, devoid of military value and requiring a minimum of skills: a few pounds of plastic explosive taped to the well-head and detonated at a safe distance – and tens of millions of dollars were up in smoke. And not just any smoke, at that, but great filthy clouds with the power to alter the weather and kill off the wildlife.

1

The stories told by those who stayed behind reinforced the impression of Iraqi bestiality. If we had any doubts about the general truth of them, one glance at the mutilated corpses in the morgue trays at the al Adan hospital was enough to convince us.

On the first night after the Liberation I stayed in a room that had formerly been occupied by a Baath party official. He had clearly left in a hurry. His clothes were still in the cupboard. They were the type favoured by secret policemen and workers in the repression business all over the region: curiously skimpy suits in brown and blue, slip-on shoes with pimpish pointed toes and club-striped polyester ties. In the bathroom two giant bottles of Old Spice sat by the sink. In the early days of the invasion their owner had no doubt been delighted to be assigned to be involved in the enterprise. He seemed to be a youngish man. The experience would be an opportunity to impress his superiors and accelerate his progress up the party ladder.

I did not have to have met my predecessor to know what he was like. I had come across his counterparts many times before. Sometimes they were polite, even charming; sometimes surly and threatening. What they all shared was a taste for bullying, a wish to corral other human beings into the pens staked out by their own masters. This dedication to distorting or reversing the truth was evidenced by the newspaper left in the unknown Baathi's room which announced on the masthead that it was the organ of the nineteenth province of Iraq, known to the rest of the world as Kuwait.

Who knows what was his rôle? Perhaps he was at the sharp end of the occupation business, supervising the interrogation, torture, murder of resistants. Perhaps it was something more mundane, such as organising efforts to impose Iraqi bureaucracy on the emirate.

Whatever his job, when he left it he had clearly been fleeing for his life. I'd had the impression as I walked through the door that the coathangers were still swinging in the wardrobe. The suits and the pimp shoes would be prized possessions in Baghdad, but they had been left behind. Only one look into the backs of the fleeing vans and lorries blitzed by the Americans on the Basra highway at Mutla Ridge revealed that the invaders had pathetically low notions of what was valuable. Inside one Japanese pick-up there

2

was a cheap metal office desk and a couple of swivel chairs: two men lay dead by the side. Even when they knew the allies were at the city gates, the driver and his companion had wasted precious minutes loading their booty into the getaway vehicle. This pitiful greed appeared to have cost them their lives.

Looking at the corpses scattered around, I wondered whether the unknown Baathi was among them. The answer was almost certainly negative. Saddam had given the orders for the functionaries to get out first, a full day ahead of his troops. In the gangster political structure of Iraq, the first priority is to save the men in suits.

The dead on Mutla Ridge were from the herd. A lot of them were middle-aged, though it is hard to judge age in Iraq where thirty-year-olds often look closer to sixty. Some of the recognisable ones were unshaven and in dirty uniforms. Many of the corpses were charred to cinders, only discernible as human remains because of an unburned boot.

The allied firepower had certainly produced some memorable effects. In the cab of a devastated lorry the driver and his passenger were mummified like Pompeians caught and stylised in their moment of death, arms thrown back in a gesture of agony. On the back of the truck was a jumble of roasted bodies. The lorry, only a few miles out of Kuwait City, had already become a tourist attraction. A little traffic jam had developed where Kuwaiti sightseers had parked their cars and climbed out with their video cameras – which had strangely escaped the looting – to record the scene. One grinning man in an immaculate white *dishdasha* took up a position behind the tangle of corpses, and waved a Kuwaiti flag, while his friend filmed him. In that instant, sympathy for the Iraqi dead finally broke through the surface of my previous indifference.

The exhausting pattern of atrocity and reprisal means that one's emotions are constantly in a process of readjustment in the Middle East. The Israelis massacre some Palestinians. A maddened Palestinian knifes an old Jewish man to death. 'Right' rarely stays on one side for long. But the speed with which Kuwait set about besmirching the image it had managed to build up during the months of occupation was surprising even by regional standards.

It was clear within a few days that a mindless *epuration* of

3

'collaborators' was about to begin. Also, that the months in exile had done nothing to diminish the arrogance and selfishness of the al Sabah family. On the other side of the border a more terrible realisation was dawning as the allies stood back and allowed the Republican Guards to move against their own people and smash the Shiite rebellions in Basra and the South.

In retrospect it was foolish to have expected that things would be otherwise and that the war would change anything for the better in the region. Nonetheless, presidential talk of a new world had presented the enterprise as a crusade, inspired by a spirit of justice that transcended *realpolitik*. In the event *realpolitik* reasserted itself immediately the United States' essential war aims were realised, and with a suddenness that astonished even the Iraqis.

Last June, during a visit to Baghdad after the war, I was on several occasions approached by ordinary Iraqis who were risking at least their liberty by talking to a Westerner. They asked why the allies had not pressed on to Baghdad. In their minds, total defeat and occupation were a far lesser evil than the continuation in power of the Baathist regime. The answer to their question was that presiding over a shattered Iraq was too much trouble, and that a weakened Saddam suited Washington better than having to deal with the chaos that would probably follow his overthrow. You might expect Iraqis to have worked this out for themselves. But many there had accepted the American justification for the adventure and believed that the cause of liberty, on behalf of which the United States had launched the biggest military operation since Vietnam, might extend to them.

In terms of serving the strategic and economic interests of the United States the war was undoubtedly a success. It had the added benefit of restoring martial pride, damaged by the failures of Vietnam, and generating an atmosphere of self-congratulation that has for the moment discouraged any too-negative interpretations of the episode.

It also enhanced the idea of collective action by the world community and in a staggeringly short time established super-power co-operation as the diplomatic status quo. And it created a sense of urgency concerning the Palestinian question – resulting in a massive effort by Washington to bring the belligerent parties to a peace conference.

For most people, though, the war was about Saddam Hussein, and the main justification for launching it was to rid the world of him. It was this prospect that sustained the American soldiers during the months of boredom in the desert. By that criterion the war must be judged a tragic failure.

On my last visit to Iraq the signs of the rebellion were visible everywhere, notably the bullet-riddled portraits of Saddam – an appalling act of lese-majesty in normal times. Nonetheless the official painters had been working hard and fresh pictures were already beginning to appear. But instead of the usual general's uniform or desert robes, the *rais* was now depicted in a white sun hat and suit, and wearing sunglasses and an ingratiating grin. The Iraqls I spoke to had no doubt what the image was saying. For the moment circumstances require a kinder, gentler Saddam. But once his strength is sufficiently restored, so too will be the evil of the old days.

PATRICK BISHOP
1991

ACKNOWLEDGMENTS

Working as a foreign correspondent means being at the end of an extended line of communication, every link of which is crucial to one's well-being and ability to work. I would like to start by thanking the invisible heroes of the *Daily Telegraph*, the telephonists and copy-takers whose calm efficiency has made life so much easier over the years.

On the Foreign Desk I owe a great debt to Paul Hill, Patsy Dryden and Theresa Jeffery for their kindness and good humour.

My gratitude is also due to Pat Prentice and Nigel Wade for their support and understanding. Above all I must thank my editor Max Hastings, an exemplary war correspondent, for his generosity and encouragement.

This is less of a history book than a memoir, a distillation of experiences and impressions during my time in the Middle East. Tribute must therefore be paid to the many colleagues and friends around the region who have generated so much wisdom and laughter. In Jerusalem, Charles Richards, Ian Black, Helen Harris, Neliana Tersigni, Bill Ries, Hugh Schofield, Patricia Allemoniere, Father Jerome Murphy O'Connor, Val Vester, Gerald and Lynn Butt, Richard and Juliet Owen, Sharon Waxman, Alain Frachon, Alia Sharwa, Ohad Gozani, Mary Curtius, Ori Nir, Michal Sella, Ivan and Mary Callan, David Winn, Shyam and Amanda Bhatia, Lucia Annunziata. In Beirut to Rudi Paulikevitch, Lena Kara, Nora Boustany, Peter and Catherine Smurdon. In Nicosia to Tim Llewellyn, Lesley Plommer, Jim and Joumana Muir, Ed and Mona Blanche, David Hirst, Mike Theodoulou, Chris Drake, Maral Aynedjian, Marianna Vrahimi, Tony and Joanna Birtley. In Saudi Arabia to Con Coughlin, David Williams, Chris Harris, Steve Back, Colin Smith, Derek Hudson and Rosemary Levine. Also to friends made along the way particularly Juan Carlos Gumucio, Jihan al Taheri and Marine Jacquemin. To all of them, much affection and thanks.

Finally I would like to express my appreciation to Gill Coleridge and Christopher Sinclair-Stephenson for ensuring that *Famous Victory* saw the light of day.

CHAPTER ONE

The Sultan Centre supermarket on the corniche in Kuwait City is an exercise in keeping the facts of Gulf life at bay. The atmosphere inside its smoked glass windows is fresh and clean, sweetened with the smell of imported fruit and spices. An escalator trundles the patrons, a mixture of locals and European expatriates, up to a first floor where the shelves are crowded with electronic goods, cosmetics and sportswear, and the counters manned with smiling, deferential Pakistanis and Indians.

On 28 July, the Saturday before the Iraqi tanks arrived, the Sultan Centre was a model of studied normality. The tills chirped and beeped. In the coffee shop, British expatriate couples with brick-red faces sat drinking lemon juice in silence. But outside – away from the air-conditioning – the unchanging cerulean sky, the burning air that clogged the lungs like talcum powder, were waiting.

Determined insouciance was the order of the day. The tone was set by the press the length of the Gulf, who had dismissed the row with Iraq as a 'passing summer cloud', that would be settled within the walls of the Arab family.

That afternoon I had tea with a young Palestinian whose father was a senior functionary in the PLO. The family had lived in Kuwait for decades and had built up a large construction business. 'You have to remember that the Kuwaitis are brilliant negotiators,' he said. 'They are bound to be able to talk their way out of the situation.'

Blindness to the obvious was a chronic condition in those

7

last days before the crisis. On Friday I had gone up to the frontier at Abdaly with two other journalists to seek information about the reported Iraqi deployment of 30,000 troops on the other side of the border. On the desert road north there was no sign whatsoever of any movement of Kuwaiti troops. When we got to the border-post – a large concrete structure with an undulating roof intended as a half-hearted nod to Arabic architectural style – virtually everyone coming into the country said they had noticed nothing unusual on their journeys, although one man said he had seen some soldiers twelve miles from the frontier.

The border guards were bored and irritable and far more interested in us than in anything that was happening in Iraq. Within ten minutes of our arriving they had been tipped off about our presence by a public-spirited Kuwaiti we had been questioning. It was time for some diversion from the tedious business of waving through lorries. First they took away Juan Carlos Gumucio, then *The Times* correspondent in Beirut. When we tried to find out what was happening we, too, were arrested. The guards were particularly concerned with Juan Carlos. His beard, Lebanese-accented Arabic and Bolivian passport gave him some genuine potential as a subversive. For some time they debated his case in front of him. For a few anxious minutes they considered the possibility that he was a Palestinian illegal immigrant and discussed among themselves whether they should send him across the border to Iraq.

After a number of phone calls to the Ministry of Information, the guards reluctantly abandoned the game, accepted that we were journalists and sent us on our way. One of them told us we had been wasting our time. There wasn't going to be an invasion.

The only place where we encountered anything other than unalloyed optimism was in the residence of the British ambassador, Michael Weston. On Saturday evening he invited the British journalists to dinner with other members of the mission. He was surprised when he was told that we were all planning to leave the following day, wondering whether it would not be more prudent to wait until the outcome of the talks in Jeddah, called to settle the dispute, that had been arranged for the following week. We left nonetheless. In the plane we discussed the seriousness of the threat. The common view was that in the Middle East politics is usually conducted like coitus interruptus, endless crescendos that rarely if ever result in a satisfactory climax. Extravagant language is the norm, whether in the service of soothing or threatening. Despite the general climate of violence there is also a finely tuned instinct that prevents even the most seemingly fanatical and irrational groups and individuals from plunging the region into the mayhem constantly discerned on the horizon.

Living in this climate, of predicted disasters that prove chimerical, impairs one's ability to spot the real thing. But in fact there were very good reasons why Saddam would not move beyond his scimitar rattling. The dispute appeared essentially to be about oil and money. It had first surfaced during the Arab League summit in May 1990. The meeting had taken place in Baghdad, after some energetic lobbying by the PLO, a choice that was intended to underline Saddam's claim to be the leader of the Arab world and a successor to Nasser. He had used the occasion to pursue complaints already made in private that Iraq was being abused by the Gulf States who were not only refusing to acknowledge the debt they owed Iraq for stemming the Iranian revolution during eight years of war, but who were now also conspiring to destroy its enfeebled economy by exceeding their oil production quotas, pushing down prices in the process. Kuwait and the United Arab Emirates were singled out for especially harsh criticism.

The charges were specified in a letter delivered to the secretary general of the Arab League on 16 July by the Iraqi foreign minister Tariq Aziz. The text was a classic piece of Baathist logic-chopping. It started with a general statement of Pan Arab sentiments declaring that 'the Arabs . . . are one

9

nation and that what belongs to them should belong to all and benefit all and that what hurts one of them hurts all.' It went on to state that despite 'all that the Arab nation suffered during the Ottoman period, then under the yoke of Western colonialism in terms of contempt, divisions, repression and attempts to distort national identity, the components of its unity have remained solid and alive.' Later Iraq was to use the fact that the Ottoman *vilayet* of Basra included modern Kuwait in order to back its claim to the territory.

Then the charges began. The Kuwaiti government, the letter declared, 'not only contradicts the nationalist principles we have just mentioned but threatens their very existence . . . the Kuwaiti leaders have undertaken methodically and knowingly to harm Iraq, attempting to weaken it at the very moment when it was emerging from a terrible eight-year war.' And Iraq was further menaced by a 'savage Imperialist-Zionist plot' because of its 'nationalistic position in defence of Arab rights'. This was a reference to the furore that had greeted Saddam's statement in April that he was the possessor of chemical weapons that would burn up half of Israel if it ever threatened Iraq.

The letter then went on to detail the elements of the conflict. It mentioned the outstanding border dispute which diplomatic efforts of the 1960s and 1970s had failed to resolve. Far from seeking a solution, it claimed, Kuwait had been using Iraq's preoccupation with the war with Iran to build oil installations on Iraqi soil. And in the preceding few months Kuwait had moved to undermine the war-damaged Iraqi economy by exceeding oil quotas agreed at OPEC and driving down the price of oil. Every time the market rate for a barrel of crude dropped by one dollar, it cost Iraq a billion dollars over a year. Not content with these unneighbourly acts the Kuwaitis had also been systematically sucking oil from the southern part of the Iraqi oilfield at Rumailah to the tune of 2.4 billion dollars.

The letter went on to affirm Iraq's right to recover the

sums stolen from it and demand reparations for the damage it had suffered. Kuwait's behaviour, it declared, amounted to 'a double aggression against Iraq: first by seizing part of her land and her oilfields and then by despoiling her national wealth.'

All in all, the passage concluded ominously, 'such an act can be compared to an act of military aggression.'

Despite the language there was much to suggest that the letter was essentially an extortion demand that Kuwait could be expected to give in to eventually. It read like a heavy-handed invitation to a negotiation the outcome of which could be in no doubt. But at least there was a little room for manoeuvre. In one passage it compared the massive loans made by the Gulf States to Iraq, during the war with Iran, to American aid to the Soviet Union during the Second World War. Did not logic dictate, it mused, that these countries should not only write off Iraq's debt in the same way but also introduce some sort of Arab Marshall Plan to help compensate Iraq for some of the losses it had suffered in the war?

If successful, Saddam stood to improve his country's fortunes dramatically, and the chances of success by a combination of bullying and self-pitying appeals to the rest of the Arab world seemed good. The use of force, on the other hand, would surely be counter-productive. Arab countries did not invade each other. It was one of the few political taboos that existed in the region.

As long as the talking continued it seemed that Saddam would get his way. Privately, Kuwaitis were saying that the government had already taken a decision to concede the demands and was even prepared to go as far as granting a leaseback arrangement on the islands of Bubiyan and Warba – the scorpion-infested mudflats in the northern gulf, long-coveted by Iraq because they overlook the Iraqi port of Umm Qasr and the strategically vital Shatt al Arab waterway.

*   *   *

11

On returning to London, I was asked by the editor of the *Daily Telegraph*, Max Hastings, whether there would be a war in the Middle East. I automatically assumed he meant a war that would be caused by the huge influx of Soviet-Jewish immigrants into Israel. This was the issue that had been exercising the whole Arab world. Indeed Soviet immigration had dominated the agenda at the Arab summit in Baghdad when Saddam had first amplified his grievance over Kuwait.

In the early hours of the following morning, 2 August, the Iraqis invaded. The Kuwaitis had done virtually nothing to defend themselves, believing that moving troops to the border would be interpreted as a provocation. The royal family fled by helicopter and limousine to Saudi Arabia. The Western papers the next day carried accounts of how one member of the al Sabah family, the Emir's half-brother Sheikh Fahd, had gone down fighting. He had been shot dead, the obituaries said, rifle in hand, while defending the Dasman palace. On a later visit to Kuwait I heard a different story from members of the opposition. Their version was that Sheikh Fahd was killed when he returned to the palace after a night out, unaware that the invasion had taken place.

The occupation of Kuwait seemed a stupid move, difficult to explain even by Iraqi logic. The state propagandists appeared to have problems concocting a justification, finally resorting to a claim that the troops had moved in to support an uprising by young revolutionaries. This fiction was soon dropped. The invasion seemed bound to prove a devastating setback for Saddam's long-term strategic ambitions. The overwhelming necessity for Iraq was to recover from the physical and economic exhaustion of the war. For this the government depended on the co-operation of the West. Iraq's relations with the outside world were already under severe strain because of the regime's unrepentant brutality. As long as this was directed at Iraqis alone, countries like the United States, France, Italy, West Germany and Britain, who had a profitable business relationship with Iraq, were prepared to mute their criticism.

But with unhelpful candour, Saddam insisted on advertising the nature of his rule. In March 1990 he had ignored a wave of appeals for clemency and approved the judicial murder of Farzad Bazoft, an *Observer* journalist accused of being a spy. This and other human rights offences were not sufficient in themselves to isolate Iraq, but coupled with the regime's obsessive attempts to acquire doomsday military technology, and Saddam's boastful declarations of his willingness to use it, they pushed the country further and further beyond the pale. The invasion removed it altogether from the domain of international acceptability.

If Saddam had much to lose he believed he also had much to gain: if he succeeded in hanging on to Kuwait he would control a massive chunk of the world's oil reserves – making him the undoubted head of the Arabs, and an important player on the world stage. The acquisition of oil and the subsequent strategic benefits, Saddam's son Oday revealed after the war, were what drove him on. What he failed to realise was that it was precisely because of the richness of the prize that the rest of the world could not let him keep it.

For a short time, though, it seemed that Saddam might pull off his coup. In the first hours after the invasion his fellow Arab leaders were frozen by indecision. Throughout the previous decade they had by and large accepted Saddam's claim to be the defender of the Arabs from the Iranian fundamentalist hordes. His megalomania had inspired a mixture of fear and admiration. Several states were linked to Baghdad by alliances. Egypt, Jordan and Yemen were fellow-members with Iraq of the Arab Co-operation Council (ACC), and Saudi Arabia had signed a non-aggression pact with Iraq.

For a day they dithered while King Hussein of Jordan attempted to prevent the outside world from interfering in the dispute and to settle the matter by fraternal Arab mediation-efforts alone. But the invasion had provided crushing proof of both the hollowness of the rhetoric of Arab brotherhood and the total inability of the Arab world to police itself.

On Friday 3 August 1990 the Arab League meeting in Cairo voted to condemn the invasion. Kuwait's fellow-members of the Gulf Co-operation Council demanded the immediate withdrawal of Iraqi troops and the Egyptian Foreign Ministry described the occupation as 'a clear violation of international law and principles of legitimacy.'

Of over twenty league members, all but Jordan, Yemen, the PLO, Libya and Sudan had voted for the motion.

The following night I arrived in Cairo. At the Hilton Hotel on the banks of the Nile, the lobby was crowded with Kuwaitis who had been on holiday at the time of the invasion. At least half their countrymen were in the same position. They wore their Gulf garb of beautifully ironed white *dishdashas* and *qutras*, and carried expensive worry beads in their right hands. In one corner of the hotel was an old-fashioned Reuter's machine. A group was permanently clustered around it, snatching each bit of copy as it clattered off the wire, studying every word for some sign of hope. The Egyptians were not overly sympathetic. The management of the hotel announced that the Kuwaiti dinar, which a few days before had been a rock-hard currency in the region, was no longer acceptable to settle bills.

Egypt was in a difficult position, a friend of both the invader and the invaded. Following the invasion, President Mubarak had made a swift decision as to where his country's interest lay. There were personal reasons for his choice. A few days before the attack was launched, Saddam had assured him that he'd no intention of moving troops into Kuwait, an assurance that Mubarak then made public. He had also been abused by Saddam at a meeting of the ACC earlier that year and accused of being a lackey of the Americans.

It was clear from the Egyptian press that the invasion was

14

regarded as a momentous event, and that Egypt's reaction to it would be of crucial importance in shaping its own future. Great store was being set by the fact that the occupation ran so contrary to the great tides that had been washing across the world in the previous year. The action had a medieval crudeness that seemed jarringly out of place. Already the invasion was being presented as a test of global political trends. Was the liberation of Eastern Europe and the collapse of communism the start of an inexorable progress towards universal political liberalisation? Or was the Middle East impervious to such international mood swings? One newspaper lamented: 'While the world is increasingly embracing dialogue and exchange of views as the proper approach to iron out disputes, the Arabs have abysmally failed to translate into reality their much publicised slogans of solidarity and unity.'

There were few direct references to Saddam. But ordinary Egyptians seemed to be in no doubt as to who was the culprit. I was driving along in a taxi when the driver pointed out a long, red wall, impressively high with a rich forest of eucalyptus trees beyond. 'It is the mad people's house,' he said. 'First Mr Begin was there. Then Mr Gaddafi. Soon Mr Saddam is coming.'

But among the intellectuals there was ambivalence. Mohammed Sid Ahmed, a Cairo leftist and newspaper columnist, said he believed that these mixed feelings would be shared by the 'masses'. 'It is not black and white,' he said. 'On the one hand there has been a lot of frustration at the sheikhdoms and the arrogant way they behave. On the other hand there are those who argue that Saddam is offering the Israelis the best gift imaginable. How can we talk about a peaceful settlement with Israel when we can't achieve a peaceful solution between Arab nations?'

Sid Ahmed was unhappy with the comparisons being made in the West between Saddam Hussein and Hitler. There was another analogy from German history: in some

15

ways Saddam could be seen as a Bismarckian figure, seeking to forge a powerful entity out of a cluster of petty states.

A few days later I left for Jordan. On the plane the man in the seat next to me was reading a Jordanian paper, *al Rai*. There was a cartoon on the front page of Uncle Sam crouched down on all fours, his tongue grotesquely extended in a vain effort to reach a barrel of Arab oil. Out of the sky a hand, presumably Saddam's, was poised to cut it off.

This was a novel interpretation of the situation. But it was an accurate reflection of the contortions of logic by which Jordanians were managing not only to fail to condemn the invasion, but also to see it as a desirable development. On the road into Amman I passed a number of cars in which posters showed the jowly, blue-chinned features of Saddam alongside a portrait of King Hussein.

There was something shocking about the zeal with which Jordan came out for Saddam. The kingdom was known as one of the more comforting spots in the Middle East. Amman always had a pleasantly provincial feel with its clean tree-lined streets, its intelligent and well-mannered population. There was none of the menace of Baghdad, or the expectation of violence that hangs in the air in Beirut and Jerusalem. Local society is touchingly eager to keep up with the West. The shops are full of third-world copies of first-world clothes. Fads that took off in Los Angeles would eventually fall to earth in Amman some years later, altered somewhat in transit, probably long discarded in their place of origin but enthusiastically embraced by the population nonetheless.

The place was imbued with the strangely suburban ethos of the palace. King Hussein had long lost any of the mystique attached to his Hashemite forbears. His enthusiasms are those of a philistine Jeffrey Archer hero – fast cars, speedboats, horses. His consort, Queen Noor, whose cool good looks and relentless charm have made her an icon of royalty-worshipping photo magazines, is a similarly modern figure. Jordan was in the front of the Middle East's hesitant moves towards democracy. Elections had been held in November 1989 in which ominously, Islamicists had emerged with thirty-five per cent of the seats and had won a number of cabinet posts. The Jordanian press theoretically enjoys a degree of freedom, although in general the newspapers and the television remain slavishly devoted to promoting the royal cult.

It has often been pointed out that the sense of stability in the kingdom was illusory, Jordan being an artificial imperialist creation carved out of the sand by the British as a reward to the Hashemites for their revolt against Ottoman rule during the First World War. The cataclysmic birth of the state of Israel and the 1967 war distorted the country's demography, creating a Palestinian majority of about sixty per cent of the population. The increasingly exigeant presence of the PLO in the kingdom led to a violent confrontation with the Jordanian army and the expulsion of the PLO in Black September 1970.

Since then relations between the King and the Palestinians and the PLO were delicate. In recent years he won their approval by his strong support of the uprising in the occupied territories and by renouncing Jordan's claim to sovereignty of the West Bank, thus clearing the way for the declaration of a Palestinian state by the PLO. In his reaction to the invasion, the King was going to have to take account of Palestinian feelings. There was no doubt where they lay.

After arriving in Amman I telephoned a Palestinian friend. She was a woman of fierce intelligence, educated in the United States and the Soviet Union, a fluent talker and writer in English. She seemed in a strangely exalted mood. 'Arabs are fed up with the Gulf States which have sided with the Americans and who don't do enough for the Palestinians or the poor Arab countries,' she said. It was the same message as the *al Rai* cartoon and one that would be heard from many Jordanians, whether Palestinian or not.

One day I was lying by the side of the Intercontinental

pool when I overheard a conversation coming from the neighbouring sunbeds. Two young Jordanian women, talking in perfect American, were discussing whether or not they would return to the United States. 'I don't think I can do it, I'm so disgusted at the way Bush has behaved,' said one, languidly readjusting her gold chain to apply some more Ambre Solaire.

A few hundred yards down the road, poorer Jordanians were demonstrating their solidarity with Iraq. The Iraqi Embassy sticks out from its surroundings thanks to a Disney-world castellated gate-house, haphazardly constructed a few years ago and a small example of Saddam's *folie de grandeur*. Within a few days of the beginning of the crisis, a little crowd could be seen permanently clustered around the metal grille where visa forms, and sometimes even visas, are dispensed. The crowd consisted of men of all ages, volunteers seeking to go and fight alongside Saddam's forces. Among them was Abdel Halim, fat and fortyish, who had taken the morning off his work at a government office to rally to the flag. He was chain-smoking Marlboros as he waited for his visa application form.

'In our minds there is no border between Iraq and Jordan,' he declared, emphasising the point with small jabbing motions of his cigarette. 'We are one country. An attack on Iraq is an attack on Jordan.'

Mohammed, a thirty-two-year-old draughtsman, nodded in agreement. 'We want to show the Americans that they cannot come here. If they turn up in the Gulf they will find the whole Arab people facing them.'

Next to him eighteen-year-old Ahmed, with a nascent Saddam moustache, piped up, 'It is our right to fight.'

Among the group of fifteen or so gathered on the hot pavement was an old Palestinian man who had been forced to flee from his home in Jerusalem after the 1967 war.

He was a model of respectability in his clean white shirt, well-pressed trousers and carefully combed hair. He was the sort of worldly, educated Palestinian that in more normal times you might seek out to get some balancing ballast of good sense after talking to the youth at the forefront of the *intifada* in the occupied territories. But this man was talking like one of the *shebab*.

His eyes were watering with emotion. 'For years we have been waiting for a chance to prove ourselves,' he said. 'Saddam has cleared our hearts and our spirits. They say he kills people but he needs to be strict if he is to be serious. The British and the Americans have always tried to prevent the Arabs from being serious. But now we have Saddam.'

He was with his son-in-law, a Palestinian with Iraqi citizenship, who was trying to get back to Iraq to rejoin his reserve unit. 'Let him through, he needs to go back to the army or he will be put in prison or shot,' the old man shouted. The crowd moved obediently aside.

Whether the volunteers ever fired a bullet or got into an Iraqi uniform is a question that was never answered. Certainly, some of them got into a fight. Some weeks later an Italian journalist went to one of the recruiting centres, set up to process the volunteers, to interview some of the would-be soldiers. Within minutes he had been wrongly identified as an American and set upon. He was beaten so badly he had to spend several days in hospital where he was compensated by a bedside visit from the fragrant Queen Noor.

Walking back from the Iraqi Embassy, I passed the American Embassy where a group, mainly of well-dressed women, were holding neatly lettered placards denouncing the American decision to send troops to the Gulf. At the side of the Embassy was a rather bigger gathering of Jordanians queueing up to get their visas to go to the United States.

It was a phenomenon already jeeringly noted by American right-wingers. But many Jordanians could see no contradiction in this. Despite the general atmosphere of prosperity and well-being, it suited these Jordanians to lump them-

19

selves in with the oppressed and the deserving of the world. At one level this was a reflection of the fact that so many were Palestinians who retained a refugee mentality even though they might have prospered in exile.

Kuwait had been a vital source of income for Palestinians over the last twenty-five years. Many 1967 refugees had gone there to work – reaching high posts in the government and industries, and making fortunes in business. Yasser Arafat had founded a lucrative construction company there. Kuwait had been reluctant to reward their contribution to the country's growth with citizenship rights, but Palestinians had nonetheless done well by the country.

The crisis showed that this was not enough to make them feel much loyalty towards the place. Years of banked resentments burst through the surface in a spurt of puritanical venom. The Kuwaitis were presented as decadent creatures, lazy and sybaritic, who in the long periods when they were not in their own country spent their time fornicating and squandering their wealth – rather, Arab wealth – enriching the casinos of Europe.

The Kuwaitis may have let a little of the money trickle through their fingers to the ranks below in the form of wages, it was conceded. But it was not enough. Fundamentally their riches were undeserved, an accident of geology, geography and imperial history. Their duty was to spread it around among the poorer Arab nations, notably Jordan which had no oil, and among the Palestinians who had no country.

Instead Kuwait had turned its back on the Arab world in favour of the Americans. In Jordanian, particularly Palestinian eyes, hatred of the United States was at the highest it had been for years. Impatience with Washington's timorous approach to finding a settlement of the Palestinian issue had created a mood of hopelessness and rage. In 1988, after decades of dithering, the PLO had finally been induced to play its trump card – acceptance of the state of Israel – in the expectation that this would lead to serious talks with the

Americans. The subsequent contacts had been at a low level and produced few results. In May they had been broken off altogether after the Abul Abbas group, a splinter of the PLO, mounted an unsuccessful attack on beaches near Tel Aviv.

The PLO leadership reacted by moving closer and closer to Saddam, who may or may not have orchestrated the Abul Abbas raid for that purpose. Lower down there was something approaching despair. Many Palestinians regarded America as an inhabitant of Samothrace or Gaul might have regarded Rome. It was distant but its power was all pervasive, so much so that responsibility for one's personal and political misfortunes could as often as not be laid at its door. Palestinians had a schizophrenic attitude towards America's perceived imperial might. On the one side, they had a rooted aversion to imperialism, which had contributed so much to their misfortunes. On the other, only America had the leverage to force concessions from Israel on the Palestine issue. It was the question you heard from Palestinians everywhere: 'When is America going to put pressure on Israel to. . . ?' So America meddled constantly and it didn't meddle enough. It was ruthless and cunning and babyish and sentimental. It was pointlessly high-minded and it was monstrously cynical.

The Palestinians saw no harm in having a paradox of their own. At the same time as despising America they would plunder it, taking it for every hour of education, every dollar, every benefit its rich, maddening society could offer.

Thus, Saddam's aggressive and challenging attitude towards the Americans had a powerful attraction for many Palestinians. Ostensibly his brutal authoritarianism should have made him repellent to the progressives, being the quintessence of the 'Ugly Arab' of American film mythology, an image so deplored by Arab liberals. But to some extent distaste for Saddam and his regime was submerged by delight that for the first time since Nasser, an Arab leader had been prepared to stare out the arrogant and uncomprehending West.

21

Attempting to explain the phenomenon, Assad Abderahman, a leading human rights figure in the Arab world mused that 'even among Arab intellectuals the idea of democracy is not so deeply entrenched that they can ignore the authoritarian heritage they were brought up with.'

Among some Palestinians the furtive admiration that European leftists in the Thirties and Forties felt for Stalin was detectable. The never clearly stated sentiment seemed to be that he may be a brute but he was an effective brute. And he was an Arab brute.

Among the ranks of his apologists in Amman there was even one Palestinian who had had relations executed by Saddam. At one level it was possible to explain away these sentiments as proof of the depth of Palestinian alienation and despair. But at the same time one could not help feeling that Abderahman was right. The Arab world had a disturbing weakness for brutal rulers, especially those sections of it that did not have to live under the autocrat's rule.

The general feeling that Jordan was a society of victims emanated from the highest level, in fact from the royal family itself. King Hussein had a strong sense of his own misfortunes, which he believed were deserving of the widest sympathy and understanding from the rest of the world.

The stock view of Jordan at this time was that it was caught between the hammer of Israel and the anvil of Iraq, and this fact determined the King's policy. The King had been an energetic supporter of Iraq during the Iran–Iraq war, helping it to export its oil. He had also pandered to Saddam's fantasies – going along with the fiction that the Iraqi leader, like the King, was descended from the prophet Mohammed.

Before the crisis the King clearly had little choice but to keep Iraq sweet. It was a policy to which America and the West had no objection. Indeed they were following the same tack themselves. After the invasion Jordan's diplomatic dilemma bristled with irreconcilable elements. It resembled the irritating Christmas-cracker game where you have to slide a number of tiny ball-bearings into plastic slots. As one rolls in, another invariably pops out.

Initially the King gave the game a try. He had not supported the Arab League motion condemning the Iraqi invasion. He had been at the forefront of attempts to find 'an Arab solution to an Arab problem', warning that any outside intervention 'could set the whole area ablaze.'

It had quickly become clear, however, that America and Britain were not going to look kindly on the fence-sitting policy that was Hussein's only real option. A week after the invasion he called a press conference to explain his position. Jordan rejected Iraq's annexation and continued to recognise the regime of the Emir. Referring to Jordan's tardiness in applying sanctions against Iraq, he said that his country 'understood fully' its obligations under the UN charter and was merely weighing up its options.

Earlier the same day, his brother Crown Prince Hassan had spoken to some of us at the Diwan al Maliki. Prince Hassan radiated a pained decency. He had studied in Britain and was a member of several think-tanks. He spoke an academic jargon of oracular obscurity which, when deciphered, spelt out the same message being heard on the streets: The Gulf fat-cats had had it good for too long.

On this occasion he was unusually concise and forceful, however. He declared there was no question of Jordan 'falling into line' to help Saddam breach the sanctions wall around him, adding flatly: 'We are not an ally of Baghdad.' The King's reluctance to join the anti-Iraq chorus, he explained, was to enable him to continue his mediation efforts.

But trying to disassociate Jordan from its old liaison with Iraq was not an easy matter. Above all there was the mood of the streets to consider. The day after the King's press conference, the Muslim Brothers called a demonstration after Friday prayers in the University Mosque in Amman, fired by indignation at the arrival of the first American troops on Saudi Arabian soil, the home of the Holy Places. In the past the organisation had been opposed to the secularist Iraqi regime. Now, vainly seeking shelter under the dusty trees from the glare and heat, the mainly middle-class crowd of about 1,000 men listened to the leader of the brothers, Sheikh Abderahhman Khalifa, call on the faithful for Holy War against Israel, the United States and Britain in defence of Iraq. Banners stretched across the palm trees were inscribed, 'Down with America the New Crusaders' and 'Train your guns against the Zionists and the Americans.' A number of young men managed to create a phoney air of menace by standing on the roof of the mosque with their heads wrapped in *keffiyehs*, the uniform of the stone-throwing *Shebab* on the other side of the Jordan. Some others helpfully burned American, Israeli and British flags. In fact they were not flags at all. No one had had the time to buy any – and where would you buy an Israeli flag in Jordan? Instead they had made them out of paper and paint. At close quarters the effect was crude. But it was good enough for the evening television news in America.

The demonstration, and the others that followed it, were clearly licensed by the palace. The King must have had many misgivings as he allowed them to go ahead. To television-led American politicians, Jordan – reliable, westward-looking Jordan – must have seemed like Teheran in 1979 that night. Yet he had little choice but to give the Islamicists their head. Some of those at the demonstration were already suspicious of his attempts to back away from Saddam. 'The King is against Saddam and the people are with him,' said Adnan Ali Mohammed, an eighteen-year-old engineering student. 'There could be a clash. The people could turn against the King.'

It was not just the Islamicists. Zeal for the Iraqi cause was breaking out in the most unlikely quarters. One day the Lion's Club in Amman abandoned its normal preoccupation with improving talks and charity dinners and urged the people to 'launch strikes against all the American and British interests and any other country which supports aggression on the Arabs.'

The safest rôle for the King to play was that of a Jeremiah. From time to time he made well-calculated nods in the direction of the street. One Sunday, sounding more like a rabble-rousing orator than a monarch, he told Parliament that the only explanation for the international community's keenness in forcing a withdrawal from Kuwait was that the industrialised nations were determined to reshape the map of the region 'in a manner that would only serve their own interests with total disregard to the Arab people's interests.' Later on he grew a beard in a display of Islamic piety.

But throughout the rest of the crisis King Hussein desisted from making specific comments on passing events and concentrated on generalised warnings about the disaster that would befall the area unless the crisis was resolved by diplomatic means.

The most immediate concern was the Jordanian economy. Cutting off trade with Iraq would have dire consequences. Having publicly stated its awarenes of its obligations under the UN charter, the Jordanian government delayed as long as possible putting sanctions into practice. Ten days after the crisis began, I went up to the border post at Ruwayshid. In one direction the road was choked with trucks carrying food, building materials, engineering parts and other loads, all bound for Iraq. From the other came a stream of tankers laden with Iraqi crude, rumbling through the desert to the southern port of Aqaba.

The Jordanians could hardly be blamed for spinning things out. The kingdom lives by export. In 1989, fifty-three per cent of its goods and services went abroad. In the same year Iraq imported twenty-three per cent of Jordan's total commodity exports and forty per cent of its agricultural and light industrial export products. On the other side of the equation, Jordan received ninety per cent of its oil from

Iraq. The *Jordan Times* calculated that complying with the blanket sanctions demanded by the UN would 'break the back of the economy already suffering from high unemployment, heavy indebtedness and huge deficits in its balances.' With the loss of Kuwait, a huge employer of Jordanian labour had also disappeared.

Since the start of the crisis the enormous army of foreign workers in Iraq and Kuwait had begun leaving, first in a trickle, then in an uncontrollable flood. Ruwayshid was where they crossed over into Jordan. Many of them had made the fourteen-hour journey from Baghdad in the back of open dumper-trucks, hungry, thirsty and sweltering in forty-five-degree heat. Some of them had had to wait ten days at the border before they filtered through to Jordan.

Within three weeks of the invasion they were passing into the country at the rate of 16,000 a day. Many of them were Indians, Filipinos and Sri Lankans who had been working in Kuwait. They were able to fly home from Amman. But by far the largest number were Egyptians, some of the estimated 1.2 million who had been working in Iraq. The Egyptian position was sensitive as their government had sided so conclusively with the United States. The Jordanian authorities wanted to keep the departees out of towns to avoid confrontations. The journey from Baghdad to Aqaba, where overcrowded ferries were constantly making the three-hour passage to Nuweibah, was taking at least four days. The road was crowded with caravans of escapers, sometimes parked at makeshift camps at the side of the road, watched over by Jordanian policemen.

The middle-class couples sat in their Chryslers and Nissans, the capacious rear seats stuffed with children and the roof racks groaning with their possessions. The poor sat on the backs of trucks dressed in stained *galabiyas*, and clutching shabby plastic suitcases bound together with string.

The Jordanians had set up a large processing centre outside Aqaba, where it was claimed that arrivals were getting through the formalities and on to a boat within six to eight hours. But sometimes boredom and irritation would set in and the crowd would become angry at the delays, only quietening down when policemen waded in amongst them wielding clubs.

The Egyptians' stoicism was impressive and uplifting. Poor, for the most part, ill-educated, facing the dismal prospect of unemployment when they got home, they displayed none of the self-pity so prevalent among the Palestinians.

One day we spent an hour talking to Egyptian labourers at a truck stop on the road from Ruwayshid. They sat at the café hungrily scooping up dishes of meat floating in greasy gravy. They showed no animosity towards the Iraqis, though they were contemptuous of Saddam and his Nasserite pretensions. Nor did they blame their own government for their plight. Most of the time they were laughing at their own delightful childish humour. 'Where are you from?' a reporter would ask. 'Argentina,' they would reply or 'Venezuela' or 'the Moon.'

One refugee was asked what he would do when he got home. He replied that he had a little money and was thinking of opening a café. 'The trouble is I have been away so long I have forgotten what Egyptians like to eat.' A disembodied voice floated out from under a stretched-out tarpaulin a few feet away. 'Food,' it said.

The refugees had at least been allowed to leave Iraq. This was more than could be said for Western contract-workers. The potential for blackmail offered by their presence had not escaped Saddam. The expatriates were about to move to the centre of his strategy for disrupting the unity of the concentric rings of international hostility that were forming around him. For this to succeed the involvement of the media was necessary. Baghdad, which until now had refused to issue visas to all but a few television stations, decided it was time to invite the journalists in.

27

CHAPTER TWO

The suddenness with which the visas had begun to flow created some alarm among the journalists assembled in Amman. By now several thousand Westerners were trapped inside Iraq, designated as 'guests' of the government. A number of them were being held at strategic sites around the country as human shields to stave off an allied attack. By going to Baghdad were we not merely adding to Saddam's stock of hostages? Adding considerably, too, as a big-name TV anchorman had twenty times the propaganda value of an oil technician from Aberdeen.

On the other hand media manipulation was clearly going to be an important part of Saddam's strategy. There would be little sense in imprisoning its members at what was clearly an early stage of something that was going to be a long drawn-out drama.

The word that the visas were ready was delivered in a phone call to the hotel by one of the functionaries at the Embassy. He spoke in the tones of a pools official informing a punter of a massive win.

Visas, the obtaining of, is a major part of journalistic life in the Middle East. As a general rule the countries that you least wish to visit are the countries that create the most obstacles to letting you in. It is not a simple matter of the undemocratic regime's dislike of Western journalists. Obstructiveness is a versatile and subtle instrument, not merely a means of control but also an organ of communication – conveying emotion, resentments, political information.

In a typical case 'X' applies to the Ministry of Information in the People's Arab Republic of 'Y' to visit the country. He is on good terms with the man who deals with the visa applications. Indeed he usually brings him a bottle of whisky and arranges for a douceur to reach him by a discreet route. On this occasion, however, he is told that there will be 'difficulties'. 'X' is disconcerted. Officials usually turn down visa applications because they don't like what you write. But the last time 'X' was in town his despatches were innocuous. The country is relatively stable at the moment so there is nothing over and above the normal torture and corruption that the authorities are particularly anxious to hide. Eventually, after many pleading telexes, the Ministry relents.

Later, sitting in the functionary's office over a cup of coffee, the real story comes out. The official's wife had been planning to go to London for an operation for some time. But though she had applied six weeks ago to the British Consulate there had still been no reply.

Arabs have a hard time getting into Europe and America. Whenever possible they make sure that Europeans and Americans have an equally hard time getting into their respective states. The Lebanese have a particularly rough ride at immigration desks. In revenge they set up a bureaucracy at the port of Jounieh – for most Westerners the usual way in before the country was pacified – that made the officials at JFK look like hopeless amateurs. Passports were examined with scrupulous intensity, with many suspicious glances darting between the fresh-faced portrait in the document and the baggy-eyed unshaven reality.

At the end of the examination the 'official', in reality a hireling of the local Christian Lebanese Forces militia, would hand back your passport with a gruff word of apology. 'No, I quite understand,' I would sometimes reply. 'It's very important to keep terrorists out of Lebanon.'

29

But here at last, after daily, sometimes twice daily trips to the gate-house of the Iraqi Embassy, was the visa – an impressively printed oblong of crested paper pasted into the book.

And so, on 26 August, we arrived at Amman airport. The Iraqi Airways desk was swamped with milling crowds of returning patriots. As usual they seemed to have bought most of their worldly possessions with them. Small, tough women piloted luggage trolleys heaped with wobbling mounds of suitcases, interspersed with cardboard boxes containing stereo cassette-recorders, microwave ovens, and the other electronic items without which no Middle Eastern journey is really complete.

They were happy to talk to journalists. Most said they were returning home because they wanted to be with their families. 'God save us from war – all of us,' said a middle-aged, middle-class matron.

Among them was an American-educated economist and his nineteen-year-old son. The young man, who had been on holiday in Britain and was going back to resume his engineering course in Baghdad even though it probably meant being called up, said: 'It is America that wants war. We don't.'

His father added: 'We love the Americans and we love the British but we don't love their leaders.' He too believed that the 'aggression' being shown by the West towards Iraq was part of a plot that had been formulated earlier in the year. Once Saddam had announced that he would retaliate with chemical weapons if he was attacked by Israel, then the campaign to destroy him began, he said.

Seen through these lenses, the invasion of Kuwait was justifiable, indeed desirable. Kuwait, too, was part of the plot. Its insistence on the repayment of war loans, its overproduction of oil and the subsequent damage caused to the Iraqi economy was the emirate's contribution to the conspiracy.

The economist's views were in line with the version of events being peddled in the Baghdad newspapers. They had been producing their own accounts of the talks in Jeddah between Iraq and Kuwait – over the question of compensation for 'stolen' oil, overproduction and the territorial dispute – the collapse of which had precipitated the invasion. They portrayed the Kuwaitis as demanding immediate repayment of the billions of dollars loaned during the war and threatening to 'raise the American flag in Basra' if they didn't pay up.

As we drove into Baghdad we heard the crackle of rifle fire. It was, it turned out, volunteers of the 'Popular Army', five-million-strong according to the unbelievable official claims, who had joined up to combat the allied threat and who were practising on the ranges. There were a few extra anti-aircraft batteries posted on the roofs of high-rise buildings. Otherwise there was little sign that the city was much affected by the crisis. The effects of the trade embargo did not seem to be being felt yet.

In the shabby, colonnaded sidewalks of Rasheed Street in the centre of town, the shops were full of goods. Giant marrows and watermelons sat in the windows of the fast-food kiosks and fruit stalls were piled with apples, oranges, grapes and dates.

As night fell the string of restaurants selling masgouf, the huge carp now mostly raised on fish farms but supposedly from the Tigris, turned on their bright neon lighting as usual. Clearly the government was reluctant to shake the mood of acquiescence towards Saddam's confrontation with the outside world by introducing early austerity measures. Along the streets and across the bridges the traffic was moving as briskly as ever. Among the Japanese imports were cars I had never seen before in Baghdad, large, boxy Chevrolet Caprice Classics. The taxi driver chuckled as he pointed them out. They were 'Ali Baba' cars, he said, looted from Kuwait.

31

The following day I drove around town. It was two years since my last visit. I had been there when Iran accepted a ceasefire in the eight-year war. Since then nothing much had changed. There were numerous new portraits of Saddam and a giant statue. It showed him in one of his favourite poses. Often on the TV news you would see Saddam arriving to inspect a new factory or review some troops. He would walk among the small throng, clearly drawn from the local party cadres and carefully screened, with his curious gunslinger's lope. Then he would raise his hand, palm upward and hold it outstretched to acknowledge the sycophants as they milled around him. Now this pose was immortalised in a twelve-foot bronze statue. One could imagine Saddam examining the drawings and models, as Hitler had amused himself with Speer's architectural plans, approving and rejecting, giving his own comments and observations to the cringing, anonymous sculptor.

If the regime was feeling any anxiety about what it had got itself into, it was not letting it show. That evening I went to see the information minister, Latif Nsayyif Jassim. He was small and dapper and fidgety. He seemed to be grappling to suppress a giggling, malign hysteria, which occasionally broke through the surface. He was an old comrade of Saddam's and was wearing the dark-green Baath party uniform. On the walls of his office were the pictures to be seen in every official's office – the occupant looking adoringly at his leader.

He was eager to talk about the Western hostages. A 'large number' he said were being held at 'vital and strategic bases' all over Iraq. He began to list them. They were air bases, military factories, oil installations, transport and communications centres, radio and TV stations, airports. . . .

I remarked that there seemed to be few places where they didn't have hostages. The minister asked the translator what I had said. Suddenly his face lit up and he cackled with laughter. 'Yes, they are everywhere. And you can be a hostage too. We will keep you here to protect the Ministry!' I smiled weakly and moved on to the next question.

Jassim was the quintessence of the Baath party thug. He lacked the education of the officials the regime normally put forward to present its case, such as Western-educated figures like Tariq Aziz. He had a threatening manner and his language was extravagant and crude.

Aziz, the foreign minister, was due to meet the UN Secretary General Perez de Cuellar in Amman in two days' time in an effort to defuse the crisis. Jassim was adamant that Iraq would not be making any concessions. 'Kuwait is part of Iraq and the al-Sabah family is finished,' he said.

At first it seemed odd that Saddam, with his highly developed sense of propaganda, should put such a man in such a position. Yet Saddam's public-relations strategy was often a bewildering mixture of good and bad judgements. The week before he had ordered himself to be filmed with a group of 'guests' including a young British boy, Stuart Lockwood. Saddam had patted him on the head and asked about his welfare. The look of fear and misery on the boy's face exposed the hideous cynicism of the occasion in a second. Instead of the fairy godfather, Saddam stood exposed as the wicked uncle.

Similarly, the regime's propaganda ploys were often remarkably clumsy and transparent. Every day there would be a 'spontaneous' demonstration outside the American and British Embassies. One day I arrived at the US Embassy to find a small crowd of respectably dressed young to middle-aged men and women outside. They were chanting slogans and waving banners written in English denouncing President Bush. They were, they explained, 'intellectuals' who had felt moved to come down and make their feelings known. A fussily tailored man with sculptured,blow,dried-grey hair was pushed forward. He introduced himself as Abdel Razzak al Majid, a poet. In fact, Iraq's leading poet, a winner of the Saddam gold medal for literature. Yes, he would be

33

happy to talk at greater length. I should come to see him at his office at the Ministry of Culture the following day. The idea that this revelation would destroy any credibility the protest might have had, seemed not to occur to the demonstrators. After a few more minutes' chanting they climbed into cars and set off to stage another spontaneous rally outside the British Embassy on the banks of the Tigris.

Even by the high standards of Middle Eastern sycophancy, Abdel Razzak was in a class of his own. He was reading Stephen Hawking's *A Brief History of Time* when we went to see him. On the bookshelf behind were leather-bound volumes of his own poetry. A paperback English translation, with his portrait on the cover, sat in front of him. His themes were love and patriotism, he said. His work had been recognised abroad. In the Soviet Union for example, and also of course at home. Indeed the President – he allowed a look of respectful devotion to pass across his face – was an admirer. One day the President had telephoned him to take issue with one of his verses. The poet had said the people of Iraq were like their own history. This was wrong said the *rais*: the people of Iraq *were* their own history. By an extraordinary coincidence the poem was included in a reading due to be given that same evening, a reading at which Saddam was to be present. Abdel Razzak had delivered the verse unaltered. 'The President's face went dark,' he recalled with a smile. 'But when it came to the end I had added another verse. A verse in which I corrected myself. The President really laughed at that.'

This story had a familiar ring to it. It illustrated a particular technique of Oriental flattery in which the flatterer appears to have adopted a dangerously unorthodox opinion. There is an uneasy moment when those around think they are witnessing a terrible *faux pas*. Then everyone is all smiles when they realise that all that is happening is that the flatterer has departed from the recognised paths of sycophancy to add some new refinement to the techniques of fawning.

In Damascus I was once promised a meeting with a Syrian dissident, a high official who had doubts about the leadership of the country and was prepared to voice them. Setting up the rendezvous was a complicated process. Arrangements would be made, then mysteriously cancelled at the last moment. At last everything was in place. I was collected from my hotel and driven to the suburbs. There, waiting for me, was a distinguished-looking man whose manner suggested a lifetime of having orders obeyed without question. For about an hour we conducted a wary, circular, conversation, expressing ourselves in the most innocuous generalities in which not a hint of dissidence was dropped. Finally I decided to come to the point. I understood, I said, that he might have some criticisms of the way the country was being run. The man moved forward in his chair in a confiding way. He looked me frankly in the eyes. 'The problem is Hafez al Assad,' he said, as my Biro began to skate across the hitherto blank page. 'What this country needs is . . .' he glanced nervously around '. . . not one Assad but ten Assads, a hundred Assads!'

Then he was away on a well-practised litany of the President's virtues. What had happened? Had he decided to unburden himself but lost his nerve at the last minute? Had it all been a misunderstanding and he had never been a dissident at all? But in that case why did he bother to see me in such clandestine circumstances!

The Assad leadership cult was a relatively restrained and practical phenomenon. Its purpose was to promote the President as a unifying figure, above the divisions and rivalries of his subjects, just as the cult of kingship had been used earlier in European history. The Saddam cult of personality was more complex and puzzling. The wayside portraits conveyed a variety of themes. In most of them he was portrayed in conventional leadership rôles, a general in army uniform or a statesman in suit and dark glasses. There were frequent allusions to history – with Saddam on horseback, often at the head of a ghostly ancient Arab army at the battle of Qadasiya, the historical victory of the Arabs over the Persians. But he was also shown as a father or beloved uncle, surrounded by children or chastely-attired women, or sitting drinking tea with a respectful group of men. All these portrayals would surely have to be submitted to Saddam for his approval. It was hard to avoid the conclusion that despite the unrelenting repressiveness of his regime, despite the pathological ruthlessness of his methods, Saddam wanted to be loved as well as feared. The fact that he was hated by large sections of the population was evident to him every minute of every day, advertised by the tortuous security arrangements to protect him from assassination. Yet the paintings of him smiling benignly, warming himself in the grateful smiles of his subjects, seemed to betray an unlikely weakness, a yearning for genuine affection.

The question of whether or not Saddam enjoyed any real popular support was one which until the very end of the crisis had been impossible to ascertain. Western diplomats would often assert that difficult though it was for outsiders to understand, there was a widespread acceptance of the necessity for harsh leadership if the country was not to drift apart and a collection of warring factions take its place. It was pointless to ask Iraqis themselves. They would invariably reply with a bland declaration of admiration and support.

The diplomatic view seemed a libel on the Iraqi people. The organs of repression were indefatigable, torturing and imprisoning those suspected of harbouring the slightest critical thought, or of having any connection with those who did, rendering dissidence a suicidal activity.

Even the most slavish mentality would revolt at the conditions imposed by the Baathists. To accuse Iraqis of actually enjoying them was the most grotesque and unfeeling condescension and, as later events showed, completely unfounded in fact.

Yet the Baathists seemed supremely confident of their continued survival. Officials scoffed at the idea that any American intervention could be the swift, surgical operation painted in the Pentagon scenarios now regularly being retailed in the American news magazines and by expert guests on the news shows. They were contemptuous of American military prowess, setting great store by the difficulties Washington had faced in Panama. 'It took eight days to deal with Noriega in a country where they had a military presence,' said one. 'What about Iraq with one million men under arms?' He went on to warn, accurately enough, that 'any attack on Iraq will provoke an attack on the oilfields they have come to protect.'

The regime also seemed unperturbed that the trade embargo would be effective enough to cause serious harm to morale, and supposed the country would still be able to feed, clothe and provide medicine for itself once the sanctions began to grip. 'What are the basic needs of the individual?' Jassim had mused. 'They are food, medicine and clothes. Iraqis don't need any new clothes for the next ten years. As for food, we have prepared the people to eat from what they produce and we can rely on ourselves for a very long time to come. As for medicine, we can produce and make medicine in our own factories.' Then he repeated a favourite observation of Baathist officials. 'The needs of the Arab individual for food and clothes are simple. The new trends and lifestyles came here with the discovery of oil.'

The idea that Iraqis, unlike their Gulf neighbours, still retained the hardiness of the pre-oil days and could exist on a diet of dates and milk would be cited after the war in support of the proposition that a new, more powerful Iraq would rise from the rubble of the conflict. The fact that Iraq had long ago given up any attempt to be self-sufficient in food and imported most of it from outside, much of it from the United States, was not mentioned.

Confidence was shored up by the belief that the hostages,

'the guests' as Jassim and his men always piously called them, were a vital diplomatic asset and one with which they could manipulate international politics and opinion to extricate themselves from their situation. The regime had announced that its attitude towards allowing foreign nationals to leave would depend on the attitudes of the foreigners' governments. The hope was clearly that as time went on individual governments would lower the level of their confrontation with Iraq in return for their citizens' freedom, thereby weakening the solidarity of the international anti-Saddam campaign. By this reckoning, the foreign media had an important part to play.

Since Iraq had opened its doors, Baghdad had been inundated with the American and European television nobility. They could be seen any day hanging around the Ministry of Information awaiting the summons that would take them to the President and to the top of the ratings. TV anchormen had come to occupy an important place in the long-distance diplomacy being conducted between the regime and the rest of the world. The propagandists of the Ministry believed that the mere repetition of their version of events would eventually swing world opinion against a military intervention. Tariq Aziz had made the offer of an open-ended dialogue with Washington in an interview with the ABC Nightline host Ted Koppel, but had been turned down. Now the Iraqis were attempting to reach the foreign public over their leaders' heads by broadcasting direct to the citizenry. The policy was co-ordinated by the smooth director of general information at the Ministry, Naji Hadithi, who had served as a diplomat in Britain before being expelled for spying. 'This is the means to bridge the gap in American public opinion, the gap created by the Bush administration's rejection of any debate or dialogue,' he said.

Hadithi was an interesting figure. He spoke witty, colloquial English, and appeared sympathetic to journalists' requirements. His urbanity led some to believe that this

38

meant he was also sympathetic to the values underpinning the Western press. In fact Hadithi was as committed a Baathist as his oafish boss Jassim. He understood perfectly the coincidence of interest between the theoretically hostile foreign media and the aims of the regime.

Journalism, especially television journalism, was motivated by competition. In terms of Iraqi coverage this meant obtaining exclusive interviews with senior figures. The biggest prize was the President himself. The American networks were in competition with each other, vying to offer the most favourable terms for the interview to take place. Eventually it was won by Dan Rather of cbs for the American networks and Trevor McDonald of itn for Britain. The results were strangely boring. Saddam was polished and polite but said nothing that had not already been imparted in official communiqués. The effect was unlikely to shake the conviction that he was bad and dangerous.

The lesser fry had to make do with Jassim who at one stage was devoting most of his day to servicing the media's needs. It still required a long wait and Japanese, French, Spanish and American crews were backed up in the anterooms of the Ministry like holiday charter jets at Gatwick, forlornly awaiting the go-ahead from the control tower.

The propaganda effort seemed to have two objectives. It was aimed at persuading the outside world that Iraq was resolute and could withstand economic strangulation and military attack. But at the same time it was signalling that Iraqis were really interested in peace.

This was where the hostages came in. Without a blush the Iraqi propagandists had inverted the situation. The detainees were presented on the 'Guests' News' tv-show, broadcast every night, as 'heroes of peace'. The implication was that they were actually co-operating in their continued detention, happy to act as a deterrent against American 'aggression'.

On Wednesday 29 August 1990 the Ministry of Information 'minders' in the Sheraton Hotel, where the journalists were corralled, were told to be up at seven the following morning to be ready to witness an important event connected with the foreign detainees. As the message was passed around it got distorted in the retelling.

During dinner that night a group of bemused Japanese journalists went anxiously from table to table asking whether it was true that all the foreign press were to be rounded up the next day and taken prisoner.

We gathered, dutifully, at seven a.m. Just as we had expected, nothing happened for hours. Then at about eleven o'clock there was a sudden flurry of activity and we were told to go to the Mansour Melia Hotel, five minutes' drive across town. The instruction was an anticlimax. We thought we were going to be taken to a strategic site out of town to interview some human shields. What we were in fact going to see were the wives and children, mostly British, of a number of men taken prisoner during the invasion of Kuwait. They included the families of British military advisers taken from their homes on the first day of the invasion.

But first there was another wait. We were herded into a room arranged for a press conference. Then an official announced that there would be a delay of about an hour. There was a chorus of protest. The official tried to quieten the pack of TV crews and correspondents, now about sixty strong, by explaining with a pained expression of humanitarian concern that the 'guests' were having their lunch. As he left the room the media mob swarmed after him only to be turned back by a phalanx of security men.

It turned out later that the proceedings were held up while the Iraqis tried to find women to talk to the press. Fear for the safety of their husbands made them highly nervous about speaking to the cameras in case it worsened their position. Yet on the other hand, here were the minders urging them to co-operate. It did not take much intelligence to realise what line they were expected to take.

Eventually a small group of women and children was ushered, dazed and blinking, into one of the hotel's reception rooms and the TV crews were let loose on them. As the journalists crashed through the doors, Hadithi looked on with an expression of cynical delight. 'Get in there!' he urged. 'Get your slice of the cake!' Amid the swirling mass of clashing camera men and sound recordists, the women managed to stammer out their stories. They had been told they would be free to leave Iraq and were now waiting for their passports to be returned and exit visas issued.

Some of them had been separated from their husbands at the time of the invasion then reunited with them at the strategic sites where they were held before being brought up to Baghdad. Among them was Mrs Glenda Lockwood from Worcester, whose seven-year-old son Stuart had been patted on the head by Saddam during the notorious televised visit to foreign families the week before. She had been taken to her husband, one of the Kuwaiti military advisers, shortly before. Speaking carefully and holding her son in her arms, she spoke the most innocuous words she could think of. 'It was a surprise to see him,' she said. 'We have been treated well. My husband is still here and I want him to come home.'

Another woman, who declined to give her name, was crying. She had been reunited with her husband for ten days before being moved to Baghdad the night before. Between sobs she said, 'We were all elated to be reunited but to be separated again is very difficult.'

A group of women had been on the British Airways flight that had landed at Kuwait airport just as the Iraqi troops arrived at Kuwait City. One of them, Margaret Hearn, who had been on her way to join her husband at a conference in Kuala Lumpur, said that when the troops arrived at the airport, they had been taken to the airport hotel and held there for four days, then half the passengers were moved into Kuwait City.

'We were divided up into groups, British, French, Germans and others, then taken to Basra and put on a train to Baghdad.' Their first stop had been the Mansour Melia, a five-star glass-and-marble complex on the banks of the Tigris with large pleasant gardens. There they were split up again. 'Our names were read out from a list,' Mrs Hearn remembered. 'They were very keen on keeping lists. We went on an hour's drive and stopped outside a building. When we got out of the bus we saw bars on the windows. We were taken inside to a room with six or seven beds.'

During the night the group was awoken and about thirty of them, men and women, taken off and driven away in a coach with tightly drawn blinds. 'They gave us a piece of paper referring to the UN trade embargo, and I got the impression that we were going to be punished,' said Mrs Hearn. Another woman who had been on that bus, a forty-nine-year-old Australian, butted in: 'We thought we were going to be killed, taken away like they took you away to the camps in World War Two.'

In fact their next destination was an office block which had corrugated iron nailed over the windows. Sometimes they heard shooting which made them assume it was an army camp. Far from being punished, however, the Iraqis were strenuously courteous and solicitous. One day a senior officer, they thought even a general, visited them. He asked if they had any complaints. When they said they would like to be able to see sunlight, he ordered the metal blinds to be removed.

One evening the guards had turned up and said that men who were not with their spouses were going to be taken away. Eleven of the group, all British, were removed. 'It was very upsetting,' said Mrs Hearn. 'We haven't seen them since.'

Later the group was held in three houses. The Iraqi captors were clearly under instruction to be on their cloyingly best behaviour. The hostages were allowed some freedom to walk around. In a sentimental gesture the guards planted a bed of roses for them. 'They tried awful hard,' said Mrs Hearn. 'We had a visit from the women's federation who wanted to know if we wanted any cosmetics. They seemed to be very interested in keeping us happy. They said we were not hostages, we were guests. But guests come and go of their own accord.'

When the group was then moved to Baghdad, eleven of their number were left behind, including five wives who had elected to stay with their husbands.

Despite the defiant talk of the Baathi officials it seemed clear that no one actually relished the thought of a fight. The importance that they attached to the hostages seemed evidence of a desire to escape peacefully from their situation. No one could have welcomed the prospect of another war so soon after the last one. The evidence of the human cost of this conflict was still all around. They were everywhere, propped up behind the fruit stalls in the markets, hanging on carpet merchants' walls, standing on sideboards in people's homes: framed portraits of smiling young men with smudges of moustaches on their upper lips in emulation of their leader. They were the sons, nephews and husbands lost in the eight years of epic slaughter.

It was only now that the government was beginning to disclose the scale of carnage, as part of its campaign to show the sacrifices it had made to defend Kuwait and the other ungrateful Gulf States from the Iranians. An official disclosed to me that 52,900 Iraqis were killed defending the Fao peninsula, a death toll of Western-front proportions. Since the ceasefire young Iraqi men had got used to the comfortable idea that they might live to see thirty. Now the prospect of being plunged back into the blood bath was looming again.

Chapter Three

Three weeks after leaving Baghdad I arrived in Saudi Arabia. The plane was due to fly to Bahrain to meet another flight to Dhahran but the air over Frankfurt was crowded and we arrived too late to make the connection. Instead the airline officials arranged to drive us to Dhahran across the fifty-kilometre causeway bridge that connects Bahrain to Saudi Arabia. The other passengers were oil-men working on contract to Aramco, which had formerly been the Arabian American Oil Company but which was now wholly owned by the Saudis. They continued to employ large numbers of foreigners, however, while the process of 'Arabisation' worked through to all parts of the system. The oil-men were all Americans. They had the sullen, resigned air of prisoners returning to jail after a weekend parole.

We reached the Saudi side of the bridge at about two in the morning. Outside the windows of the air-conditioned bus, the air was hot and wet. The customs officials ordered us to open our bags and began a painstaking search. Every item of luggage was examined in minute detail. After-shave bottles were sniffed in case they held illicit alcohol. One man had brought a home-video of his family. The officials were disbelieving. It could well be pornography, they said, and confiscated it until the contents could be checked. Unbelievably, one of our number had indeed tried to smuggle in some soft porn in the shape of a stack of *Playboy* magazines in his bag, packed among his overalls.

The officials began leafing through each one, lingering over the pages with writing on them as if to convince us of their own lack of lubricious intent. Then they confiscated them along with the culprit's passport, telling him he would have to come back the following morning to collect it. He slunk away, visibly weighed down by the thought of the bureaucratic nightmare that lay ahead.

The following day I went to the Joint Information Bureau (JIB) to register with the Saudi and American authorities. The office was set up to control the hundreds of journalists who had arrived in Dhahran and covered the whole first floor of the International Hotel. At one end of the room three TV sets were showing CNN; American servicemen and Saudis in *thobes* and *qutras* were watching with total absorption. Noticeboards announced forthcoming trips to visit the airbase, or navy ships or newly arrived troops. Clerks sat behind their desks gazing at computer screens. Between them officers walked to and fro importantly, clutching pieces of paper. A line of supplicant journalists and network fixers stood waiting to make their special requests. Some of the longer-established ones called out hopefully to their contacts in the office, ingratiatingly using first names. The servicemen behind the desk were polite but distant, managing to convey a slight air of hostility behind their motel-receptionist courtesies. It was clear from the outset of the conflict that the military's attitude towards the media was one of deep suspicion. Later on I was to learn that within all levels of the army and the Marines, from the mess-hall chow-line to the general's office, the simplistic cliché that it was the networks and the *New York Times* that had caused America's defeat in Vietnam was believed utterly.

This view, unreflectingly accepted, was at the centre of the military's media policy. The purpose of the JIB, it was immediately clear, was to present only good news and wherever it was deemed important, to exercise control, all the time protesting its belief in the right of journalists to gather and disseminate information without let or hindrance.

For the moment though the military build-up was overshadowed by events in Kuwait. That morning reports from the Saudi border-post at Khafji said that Kuwaiti refugees were once again pouring across the frontier which had been more or less closed for the previous three weeks. By the end of the day some 2,500 had crossed over. The following day I drove up to see them. It was mid-morning when I arrived and the weather was unbearably hot. Every now and then gusts of wind sweeping in from the desert would whip the sand off the surface, in a stinging, blinding spray. Beyond the immigration-post the refugees' cars, raft-like Chevrolet Caprice Classics and huge suburban station-wagons, stretched out in a glittering line of hot metal that reached five kilometres down the road. The men stood by the vehicles fanning themselves. Some of the women had moved with their children under the concrete canopy of the post. They were having to fend for themselves. Many of the refugees said they had been forced by the Iraqis to leave their Asian servants behind. From the lavatory block a nauseating stench of excrement wafted through the heat-laden air.

The story they all had to tell was pretty much the same. In the past few days, they said, Iraqi troops had spread the word around town that the border was going to be opened and it would be sensible to leave. They had not needed much encouragement. On the road they had been systematically robbed at the checkpoints by troops who relieved them of their cash and valuables. They painted a terrible picture of the occupation, of Iraqi soldiers carrying out random executions, raping and looting and destroying property.

'We don't want to leave our country but it was either do that or be killed by the Iraqi soldiers,' said a thirty-year-old aviation technician. 'They are catching men and young boys and putting them in front of their houses and shooting them. They hand their mothers or wives a piece of paper saying,

46

"We have killed your husband or son because he was one of the Kuwaiti resistance."'

The boastful propaganda claims of the Kuwaiti radio-station, broadcasting into the country from Saudi Arabia, were resulting in Iraqi sweeps through the areas which the radio identified as opposition strongholds. 'The radio says there is strong resistance in Bayan Salwa (on the southern outskirts of Kuwait City), but it doesn't exist any more. There was some in the early days of the invasion but not now. They don't have the weapons. The troops go into an area and check all the houses. If they find a hunting rifle you get the death penalty. If you have a photograph of the Emir they burn the house. If there are four men together with their families in one house, they will take two or three and either take them to Iraq or kill them.

'I saw three kids, sixteen years old, being shot dead in Salwa,' the technician went on. They caught them and said: "We think you are in the resistance." Then they shot them. They put them against the wall, covered their eyes and shot them in the head with rifles.' He appealed to the radio to stop reporting that resistance was strong, when it was now reduced to a few individual incidents.

Another man described seeing troops arrest a teenage boy whom they forced to stand on a bridge over one of the motorways that circle the city. 'They drew a line across his forehead. I was watching from a window. Five soldiers began firing at him. They seemed to be trying to shoot close to the top of his head and around his arms as close as possible. He fell down. I don't know if they hit him or he fell unconscious.'

There were several reports that a supermarket manager had been shot in front of his customers when he refused to display a portrait of Saddam Hussein. There were also stories that the Iraqis were being helped by members of the Palestinian community, who before the invasion made up about 400,000 of the population. They were driving around the city identifying the houses of officials, army officers and senior policemen of the old regime.

Many of the refugees believed that the decision to open the border was part of a deliberate policy to drive the remaining Kuwaitis out of the country to hasten the process of absorbing the territory into Iraq. Before the exodus it was estimated that there were still about 270,000 Kuwaitis left in the emirate. Almost all the refugees I spoke to agreed that as a result of the brutality of the occupation nearly everyone who could leave would and only the very old, the sick or the eccentrically stubborn were left behind. But as it turned out, a fair number did stay, even though they had the chance of escape. Indeed some Kuwaitis and Palestinians who found themselves outside the country at the time of the invasion slipped across the border to rejoin their families later on. The Kuwaitis pouring into Khafji had had enough, however, and it was hard to blame them.

Despite the circumstances, the Saudi bureaucracy was moving at its usual, unhurried pace. If anything it was slower than usual. There were fears that there might be some Iraqi agents planted among the escapers, bent on a terrorist campaign of assassination and sabotage while still inside the kingdom. As it became clear that they were unlikely to get through the frontier that day, some of the men started to put up the tents provided by the Saudi authorities. Their efforts were inept and half-hearted. The wind tugged at the canvas and the pegs refused to stay in the loose sandy ground. After ten minutes they gave up and returned to their cars.

Despite their sufferings it was hard to feel very sorry for the Kuwaitis. They sat in self-pitying groups around the Dhahran hotels, which were paid for by the Saudi government, playing with their worry beads, chain-smoking and murmuring in low voices. Upstairs their womenfolk sat in their rooms ordering an endless succession of meals from room service. In the swimming pool their charmless, overweight children yelled and splashed, oblivious to the sharp looks of the other patrons.

The government-in-exile had set up a propaganda office at the International Hotel under the guidance of an American public-relations company. The walls were covered with posters of torture victims printed in garish primary colours. I had seen the same sort of thing all over the region, in the same cheap, blotched ink and printed on the same shiny paper. Everyone with a grievance, from the Libyans after the bombing of Tripoli to Palestinian activists advertising the wrongdoings of the Israelis, had a firm belief in the power of mutilated corpses to swing opinion behind their cause. To my eyes there was always something gloating about the pictures. There seemed to be little thought for the dignity of the victim. It was like a Cairene beggar, who having long accepted his own deformity, holds up his stumps, which still have the power to shock others, and to shock to advantage.

On the road to Khafji I had caught my first sight of American troops in the field. Their broad-brimmed cotton hats and open, sunburnt faces gave them a slightly old-fashioned pioneering air like nineteenth-century rough-riders. The roads were crowded with 'Humvees', the high-mobility all-purposes vehicles that have replaced the old jeep. The Humvees were wide and squat with a huge radio antenna swaying behind them as they whined up and down the featureless coastal highway. Every day the JIB ran trips out to the desert for the journalists to meet the troops. In the absence of any real news, they were taken up eagerly.

The first trip I joined was to a support battalion of the 24th Mechanised Infantry Division. Many of the personnel were women, among them a pretty twenty-six-year-old with thick, dark hair cropped short. Her brutal haircut had failed to bring about the desired martial effect and she looked lonely and lost. Corporal Michelle Thompson was sitting on the edge of her cot reading a letter from her mother in Coldwater, Michigan and looking at some snaps of her three-year-old daughter, Shanel. 'I'm hoping that nothing happens so we can be home by Christmas,' she said. Under the canvas it was stiflingly hot and without the drying desert wind one was quickly bathed in sweat. As well as the temperature there were scorpions, snakes and poisonous beetles to contend with. Corporal Thompson, after working in a restaurant and a dry-cleaning shop, had joined up 'to do something different, to see the world.' She shared the tent with three women and eight men. 'The women are all pretty tight together,' she said. 'If the guys start picking on one of us the others will step in.'

The tent was under the command of Staff Sergeant Deborah Holland, a gruff black woman. Some of the journalists wanted to know whether there were any sexual relationships between the men and women soldiers. She explained that the official position was that 'fraternisation', as it was euphemistically called, was banned between officers and NCOs and other ranks for disciplinary reasons. It was tolerated between heterosexuals of the same rank, but not encouraged. 'We don't have anything like that here,' said Sgt Holland, cradling her M16 rifle. She had left a husband and two children behind in Germany for a tour which the unit had been told could last up to a year. She softened as she remembered her family. 'I called the other day,' she said. 'When I spoke to the children I tried not to cry. Just before I did I said, "Let me speak to your father now."'

A few days later I was taken to see a support unit of the First Marine Expeditionary Force which had set up a rudimentary camp in the desert called 'Landing Zone Foss' after a Second World War Marine hero. The occasion was a visit by the Marine Corps Commandant, General Alfred Gray. At seven-thirty three helicopters circled the camp and landed in a dramatic swirl of sand. Gen. Gray jumped down and called the men to gather round. His obligatory nickname

50

was 'Big Al', a misnomer as he was rather short. He had a lumpy, working-man's face, tobacco-stained teeth and an aggressive cocksure manner.

Seizing a loud-hailer from a subordinate, he announced: 'There will be no morale problems in the First Marine Expeditionary Force. There will be no boredom.' The Marines replied with a noise somewhere between a bark and a grunt, the recognised way of demonstrating approval.

After forty years in the Corps which he'd joined as an enlisted man, and by now addicted to 'Red Man' chewing-tobacco and a veteran of Vietnam, Gen. Gray was the antithesis of the soldier as bureaucrat. He could think of no higher calling than being a Marine. 'You are the very best that our nation has to offer,' he said. 'I'm privileged to serve with the greatest bunch of Marines the nation has ever had in peacetime. You make your commandant very proud.'

He claimed, wrongly as it was clear even at the time, that had it not been for the swift deployment of the Marines, Saddam's forces would have rolled on from Kuwait. 'The most important thing you have to remember is that you've already won a big one,' he said. 'I believe that Saddam Hussein and the Iraqi forces fully intended to invade Saudi Arabia but they didn't and they are stuck.'

In honour of the occasion a hot breakfast was served to the men. They queued up for fifteen minutes to receive a quivering dollop of egg and sausage, a spoonful of pallid potatoes and a lump of cake sparsely flecked with cherry. The Marines were grateful and the general's popularity ran high. At the end of his thirty-minute pep talk there had been a question-and-answer session which had proved rather anticlimactic after Big Al's fire-eating words. The first question was about danger-money and the second about leave arrangements. It was only the fourth Marine who asked, 'When are we going north?'

For all the talk, most minds seemed to be on what soldiers' minds are usually on. 'I don't know what I miss most,' said

Howard Schelleberger, a twenty-four-year-old medic. 'Yes I do. Women. Then beer.'

But these two things were of stellar unobtainability in the desert or indeed anywhere else in the kingdom, and the military authorities were determined that thoughts of them should be driven from the minds of the soldiers as soon and as thoroughly as possible. The troops had been issued with an elaborate list of behavioural guidelines aimed at minimising the offence their presence might cause to Saudi sensibilities. Male soldiers were told that as much as to look at a woman in the street would be interpreted as a dire insult and a deep offence to honour. Women soldiers were warned to behave with the utmost modesty and decorum. They were not allowed to drive on the main roads in keeping with Saudi custom, nor to carry guns in town.

The same booklet attempted to familiarise the military with Saudi and Islamic customs. It warned servicemen and women not to pull away in hygienic alarm if an Arab engaged them in conversation at close quarters. This was the local practice and nothing to worry about. Similarly the sight of young males holding hands was not to be misinterpreted. It did not mean they were homosexuals. All this made the kingdom appear a minefield of potential social embarrassments. It was essential when sitting down, the troops were counselled, not to show your Saudi partner the sole of your shoe, as this would cause grave offence. Neither was food or drink to be taken from an Arab with the left hand. The military advice was to be deferential and placatory in attitude towards the inhabitants of the kingdom they were defending. The guide issued to the media by the United States Information Service, was equally anxious not to cause offence. In the section on Saudi customs and laws it warned women 'not to sit in a car beside a man other than her husband', a nonsense when women made up about a quarter of the journalists covering the story.

There were early signs that, despite the extraordinary

circumstances, the Saudis were not going to tolerate any watering-down of the social restrictions applied to foreigners. At one point the wives of some Aramco workers decided to put on a concert for an audience of American servicemen in the US consular compound in Dhahran. Part of the entertainment involved a chorus-line routine. The evening was filmed by one of the American networks and broadcast on the following night's news. The Consulate was immediately informed by the Saudi authorities that no further concerts would be allowed.

Stuck out in the desert or confined to base camps, there was little contact between soldiers and Saudis anyway, so the concern for local sensibilities was to a large extent unnecessary. For journalists and servicemen in Dhahran and Riyadh, the oppressive strictures of Wahhabi Islam soon became drearily familiar. Virtually all entertainment was outlawed. There were no cinemas or theatres, nowhere to see dancing or hear singing. On the beach at al Khobar there was a funfair but it was barred to men unless accompanied by their wives and children. There were places to eat, including a very good fish restaurant, but the prospect of oysters or *hamour* without a crisp Chablis to wash them down soon dimmed the appeal.

For most people the main entertainment was milling around the shopping malls. The biggest was at al Khobar, the al Shula shopping centre. Every night the place would be full of third-world expatriates and off-duty soldiers escaping from the heat of the night in the air-conditioned cool of the shops. Mostly they sold electronic goods, cheap clothes and fast food. There were several music stores selling knock-off cassettes of Western and Filipino stars. Even here the long arm of Saudi puritanism reached in to interfere. Five times a day the minarets reverberated with the cry of the *muezzin*, strangely musical compared with that of other Arab countries, announcing the *salah*, when prayers were supposedly compulsory. If it was during shopping hours the shopkeepers

53

would then have to pull down the shutters and close the store or risk a run-in with the *mutawwa* ('Volunteers'), the state-employed religious police. Failure to shut up quickly enough could mean a night in the cells. This policy was arrogant and hypocritical. Few of the customers or merchants of the shopping centre were Muslims, let alone Wahhabis. The Saudis stayed away. The malls were the haunt of the Asians, many of whom were Catholics, getting the only respite available from their drab daily existence. A colleague, Con Coughlin, fantasised about setting up a rival religion in which zealots roamed the streets armed with breathalyser kits and carried out two a.m. raids on private houses. Anyone found with less than a bottle of wine's worth of alcohol in his blood, or who was not engaging in violent sexual activity, would be hauled away for punishment and re-education.

The economic pecking order among the expatriates was sharply delineated. The Europeans recreated a pale facsimile of the societies they had come from behind the walls of the compounds. These were suburban enclaves where pleasant bungalows sat among well-watered gardens. Drinkers could brew their own hooch called *sadiki*, Arabic for 'my friend', sportsmen could play golf on the Aramco course, or ride or play tennis. Life was dull but the pain was eased by the tax-free money piling up in the off-shore bank account.

Many of the Third Country Nationals, or TCNs as they were abbreviated to, lived in wooden townships – with cheap air-conditioners wedged into a window to combat the heat. They went home to Sri Lanka or India or Pakistan or the Philippines perhaps once every two years if they were lucky. It was vital for their families that they stayed. For the ordinary workers the rewards were pitiful. A taxi driver or a petrol-pump attendant received about three hundred dollars a month. But in the societies they had left behind, that was serious money, capable of sustaining a whole family. For all their privations the TCNs remained cheerful and brave throughout the crisis. Unlike the Europeans and Americans, whatever dark thoughts they had about the Saudis, they kept them smilingly to themselves.

Viewed from Dhahran, a war did indeed seem inevitable. Every day more troops poured in and the skies around the airbase were crowded with giant cargo planes – the giant Starlifters and Galaxys and the smaller but doggedly reliable C130s – freighting in vast supplies of ammunition and supplies. 'Inevitable' that is, unless there was a swift and unconditional withdrawal by Saddam. At one point the allies' main fear was that he would indeed pull back, perhaps not all the way but to a line drawn in front of the disputed Rumaila oilfield and which enclosed Bubiyan and Warba, namely the strategic islands which Baghdad claimed were essential to guarantee its security. This was the so-called 'nightmare scenario'. By doing so, the argument ran, Saddam could claim a moral victory that could enhance his claims as a great Arab nationalist leader. He had stood up to the combined might of the West and not been defeated. Indeed by the standards of the region he could claim a victory without fear of ridicule. The 1973 Yom Kippur war, regarded by the rest of the world as a triumph for Israel, is celebrated in Egypt as a great Arab feat of arms on the grounds that it showed that the Israelis were not invincible and at times during the conflict had come close to defeat.

Once he had withdrawn a safe distance from Kuwait City, the scenario developed, significant numbers of the Kuwaiti population and people might decide it was time to go home. The dispute would settle down into an Arab wrangle, perhaps with a UN peace-keeping force deployed on the interface, at which point the diplomatic coalition against Saddam would begin to crumble.

The United States and the Western allies would thus be left with none of their goals achieved, Saddam would still be in power, but with his army and in particular his chemical and nuclear capacities intact, his prestige enhanced and his appetite for further adventures probably increased. Allied officers in Riyadh were open about the fact that killing Saddam was a primary war aim. They were equally frank about the unwisdom of saying say so in public.

Despite the constant talking-up by American briefers of the Iraqi threat, allied military Intelligence privately had a low opinion of the quality of the troops and the strength and sophistication of their defences. The threat from chemical weapons was good propaganda. But the chances of them being used to any great effect against either soldiers or civilians was judged to be small. The Intelligence reports said that most of Iraq's long-range missiles were still sited around Baghdad and facing west towards Syria and Israel. The allies were also confident that they knew the whereabouts of all Iraq's chemical weapons stocks. If they were moved south and into range of Saudi Arabia, this would provoke an attack, the Intelligence community predicted.

Fears that a deal could be in the making were enhanced by the alarmingly pacific noises that suddenly began emanating from the House of Saud. Towards the end of October King Fahd made one of his rare utterances on the situation. During a speech of welcome to President Mubarak of Egypt on his arrival at Jeddah airport, he suggested that Saddam could pull out of Kuwait without loss of face.

'I do not see that, if a blunder were committed, we correct the mistake with another mistake,' he said. 'If President Saddam were to consider the matter seriously he would find that it is in his interest personally and in the interest of the Arab nation that he should withdraw from Kuwait.' The King added: 'A blunder has been committed . . . I believe Saddam should not think that if he returned to right, logic and reason it would be taken as a shortcoming on his part.' The King's bland description of the rape of Kuwait as a 'blunder', his respectful reference to 'President' Saddam, sent a spasm of fear through the allies that the 'nightmare scenario' was in the making, abetted by the Saudis. Only the day before the King's speech, the defence minister, Prince Sultan, had hinted that Iraq could negotiate territorial concessions from Kuwait if it first made a complete and unconditional withdrawal. Western diplomats were quick to maintain that the royal family's words did not indicate any slackening of will and suggested that in effect they were offering Saddam a last chance of a peaceful settlement before the region moved inescapably towards war. This was indeed what was happening. Three days after King Fahd's conciliatory remarks, reports from Washington revealed that President Bush was about to send more than 150,000 extra troops to the region to join the 210,000 already in place, to provide an "adequate offensive military option".

The draconian social laws designed by the Saudis for themselves seemed to bespeak a society of fierce, unruly passions which only the harshest measures could curb. The Western newspapers and magazines arriving in the country were subjected to painstaking censorship. This meant a team of men working through every copy of every publication, inking out anything that might provoke temptation. Every advertisement for whisky or wine was blotted out. The question of women was more problematical. The mere representation of a woman was not in itself offensive. A tight head-and-shoulders of Mrs Thatcher, for example, would pass muster. But beyond that lay deep and dangerous waters. Pictures of ballet dancers and the like were definitely out, occasioning the removal of the whole page. Some broad-minded censors would allow the display of a demurely shod calf. But their stricter colleagues were usually in the ascendant – slashing away with their felt tips at cleavage and ankle with righteous energy. In their rheumy eyes almost any female had the power to inflame. Lady columnists of a certain age would be surprised and perhaps flattered to know that the

57

superannuated portraits over their weekly jottings were closely scrutinised by the guardians of morality for their potential to deprave and corrupt. We never discovered the qualifications for the job of censor. Were they ascetic men of superhuman self-control? Or were they reformed debauchees skilled in identifying harmful material but in whom the fires of lust had long burned out?

It was hard to reconcile the strictness of the social code with the blandness of the Saudis one encountered in offices and hotels. There was little chance of meeting them elsewhere as their formal politeness seldom extended to inviting outsiders into their homes. Saudi men seemed stodgy and complacent, unrecognisable as the lean zealots who had followed Abdul Aziz Ibn Saud only two generations before. Their main recreation appeared to be sitting in hotel coffeeshops for hours on end making desultory conversation. The women were hardly noticeable at all. Occasionally some of the more liberated ones would appear with their spouses and children in a restaurant, only to be immediately hidden away from the eyes of male diners behind screens in one of the 'family rooms'. Otherwise they could be glimpsed, in *abaya* and headscarf, in the back of the American cars in which their husbands erratically plied the highways at all times of the day. Driving, apparently aimlessly, was one of the few things there was to do. The Saudis did it badly. They lurched from lane to lane without warning, executing left and right turns at full speed. Most drivers seemed to be engrossed in debate with the man next to them, or dreamily smoking a cigarette. The dangerous relationship between smoking and driving was one that concerned the authorities. The television regularly showed a public-information film pointing out the potential perils. One sequence showed a man finishing his cigarette and idly throwing it in the back of the car, only to be overwhelmed by smoke a few minutes later as the back seat caught fire. The film seemed to accept that a sort of childish irresponsibility was part of society.

One day, later in the year, I took my car out a few minutes after the first shower of winter had finished. In the space of a ten-minute journey I saw three wrecked cars whose drivers had been unprepared to make the slightest concessions to the changed conditions. What the roads would have been like if alcohol had not been banned defied the imagination.

Whether Saudi society, or its upper reaches, would have tolerated these restrictions if they were subjected to them all year round, year in year out, is debatable. As it was, most wealthy Saudis frequently travelled abroad and many had lived overseas for considerable periods. The Saudis themselves reckon that twenty per cent of the population visit the West every year for protracted stays. This had inculcated what they would describe as a pragmatic outlook, and what others might regard as simply hypocritical. A senior official who had lived abroad with his family for a decade told me he was happy for his daughters to drive, drink and wear mini-skirts in Europe, but would not countenance them seeking the same freedoms at home. These double standards were presented by some as an indication of the strength of Arab values. They could live abroad, taste the pleasures of Western life forbidden to them at home, but were still happy to return to the austerity of Saudi Arabia for a revitalising exposure to their traditional values. Many people I spoke to were genuinely contemptuous of Western liberalism, particularly its attitude to crime. What sort of society was it, they asked, that allowed child murderers to live or released rapists from prison to rape again?

But without the release of regular visits to the outside world, one doubts whether educated Saudis could happily withstand their own self-created society for long. The rules were never intended to apply to the upper echelons. Behind the walls of their houses, they drink and watch imported videos. The code was designed for the pious Wahhabi lower class, the herdsmen and bedouins, who accepted it happily. It was they who gave the religious authorities their power, and it was the religious authorities who underpinned the rule of the al Saud family. Therefore anything that undermines the religious integrity of the kingdom also undermines the whole social order.

From the outset there were predictions by outside observers that the American deployment, whether or not it ended in war, would prove to be a traumatic experience for Saudi Arabia. The pessimists believed that the huge influx of unbelievers, including a large number of women, into the kingdom on whose sands the sacred sites of Mecca and Medina were located would create a dangerous mood of resentment among the religious establishment, which could eventually threaten the monarch. The optimists thought that Saudi Arabia's open alliance with the West could prepare the way for reform. Certainly the rulers felt compelled by the new situation to show a more open face to the West, at least for the duration of the crisis. The King and the ruling princes understood that if the United States were to go to war in the interest, albeit shared, of their country, then the kingdom would have to present itself as a worthwhile cause.

Hitherto Saudi Arabia had been virtually closed to journalists. Those reporters who got there, usually business or oil specialists, found officials secretive and information hard to extract. The new circumstances dictated that the government would have to relax its habitual and instinctive secrecy. For this purpose they decided to activate officials more familiar with communicating with Westerners and charged them with a mission to explain. Among the most visible was Prince Mohammed Bin Feisal Bin Turki, who was responsible for Islamic affairs at the Washington Embassy.

Prince Mohammed was baffled by Western interest in the ban on women drivers. 'It's not an Islamic thing, it's more of a social and cultural thing,' he explained. You don't change the whole sociological set-up of society just because you disagree with it.' As for Western-style democracy, he said simply: 'It is not suitable for Saudi Arabia. This government bases its legitimacy on its commitment to Islam and its application of Islamic law and this is what made the country what it is today.'

At one level the invasion and the attention it focused on Saddam's regime made the propagandists' work easier. The glaring awfulness of Iraqi Baathism made the repressiveness of other governments seem trivial in comparison and provided officials with a further justification for the continuation of the system. 'We're not a paranoid society like Iraq or Syria,' said a young, Western-educated diplomat. 'We're not a police state disguised as a democracy.'

The idea that through exposure to Americans, Saudi Arabia might somehow catch democracy, like a sort of benign flu, was a Western view. Even the most liberal-minded Saudis were sceptical that the deployment would prove the catalyst for social or political reforms inside the country. The kingdom had lived with large numbers of foreigners since oil began being pumped and had successfully contained and isolated them. The Western armies presented a larger problem, but given the allied desire to be in and out of the country as fast as possible, probably a temporary one.

What the Saudi progressives did hope was that the leading rôle that the kingdom had been forced by events to take might continue once the crisis was resolved, and that Saudi Arabia might prove a new, pragmatic force in formulating the order that emerged from the upheaval.

One day I had lunch with a young diplomat from the Washington Embassy who had been brought back to act as a press-liaison officer. He was wearing a *qutra* and *thobe*, but he had on trendy wire-rimmed glasses such as you see on young New York corporate lawyers. They glinted as he leaned over the table and said gleefully: 'Pan-Arabism is finished! Saddam Hussein has burst the bubble. It was all fake anyway. Arab nationalism died in 1967.' He went on to make a list of predictions for the aftermath of the war that would have pleased the Israeli cabinet. King Hussein

61

would be toppled in Jordan, he said, and there was a possibility that the Arab-Israel conflict could then be resolved by handing over the country to the Palestinians.

The days of no-strings donations by the Saudis to Arab indigents, who often came with one hand outstretched and the other waving a v sign, were over, he said. 'In the future Saudi aid will be distributed for reward or punishment.' The PLO, he thought, 'is finished as a political force. It doesn't have any credibility any more.'

Underlying these hitherto unsayable views was a deep dismay at the Arab failure to capitalise on its advantages and a consequent loyalty to the Saudi rather than the Arab nation. The invasion had finally exposed the flatulent worthlessness of the Pan-Arab rhetoric that had been wafting the politics of the region hither and thither for the preceding forty-odd years. For a brief period officials were enjoying the luxury of speaking their minds, although anonymously.

And if the Saudis were having to re-examine their image in the eyes of the outside world, the problem was even more pressing for the Kuwaitis. Since their flight the al Sabah family and its ministers had set up home in Taif, a resort in the hills behind Jeddah. Their centre of operations was in a luxury hotel a little way out of town. Several rooms were occupied by representatives of the American public-relations firm that was nurturing the al Sabah image. When I arrived there one day in the middle of October the government was preparing to move down from the mountains to the coast – for the first serious test of its popularity since the invasion. Kuwaiti exiles were holding a three-day conference at which about 700 delegates were to discuss a liberation strategy for their country and also the manner in which it should be governed once it was freed. The conference was officially sponsored. It was presented as an example of Kuwaiti democracy, a response to popular pressure for a general stock-taking of the situation. There was no doubt that it was also aimed at reassuring American public opinion about the nature of the government that its sons and daughters were preparing to shed their blood to restore.

Before it began government ministers put forward for interview emphasised Kuwait's democratic credentials. 'I think our system is more or less the same as the British,' said Yayha al Sumait, the minister of housing. 'We have the parliament, the constitution and the free press.' In fact Parliament was dissolved in July 1986, the subsequent elections for a consultative assembly had been boycotted by the opposition and the press was slavishly pro-regime.

Despite the official nature of the gathering, a number of opposition figures were among the delegates. There was a possibility that they might use the media interest to publicise their cause. In the event, though, nobody seemed keen to rock the boat by pursuing old grievances. The pro-democracy parliamentarians insisted that they were fiercely loyal to the al Sabah family. 'We are just trying to restore the constitution and the parliament,' said Ahmad Saidoun, the former parliamentary speaker and a focal figure for the opposition movement.

In fact the Kuwaitis had put on a remarkable display of solidarity since the invasion. There had been no reports of widespread collaboration among those who remained in the country (about a quarter of the 650,000 indigenous population) and passive resistance appeared to be solid. Those outside had refrained from recriminations and backbiting. Indeed their allegiance seemed to have hardened around the sixty-four-year-old Emir, Sheikh Jaber, and the rest of the al Sabahs who controlled one third of the government posts. 'I have not met one person who is speaking about him in a negative way,' said Mr al Sumait. 'We don't want any ruler other than the al Sabah family.'

Their flight, far from being a target for criticism, was being presented as the statesman-like thing to do. It was for this reason, I initially thought, that the propagandists were so reluctant to play up the rôle of Sheikh Fahd, who according to the first stories had gone down in a blaze of glory defending the Emir's Dasman palace in Kuwait City from the invaders.

'The legitimacy has not been eroded in any way,' said Abdel Hadi al Otaibi, one of the delegates who had been a scientist at the Kuwait Institute for Scientific Research before the invasion. 'If the Emir had stayed he would have been caught and executed, knowing the way of the Iraqis. Then there would have been no legitimate government.'

At the same time there appeared to be very little criticism of the lack of military preparedness by the government – which had made no move to reinforce Kuwait's borders after the Iraqi build-up. 'If the army had defied the invasion it would have been only a matter of hours before it would have been crushed,' said one minister.

When the Emir shuffled into the room on the Saturday afternoon – a shy, nervous-looking figure – he was received with rapture. Yet behind the display of loyalty in the corridors and the coffee shop there was a widespread acceptance that the family had a moral duty to restore the old constitution once they had been returned to power. When this might be was by no means clear. 'After the invasion I thought we would be back in a fortnight,' said an engineer stranded in London when the tanks rolled in. 'Now the longer it goes on the more pessimistic I get.'

At the same time most of the Kuwaitis were convinced that the stand-off between Saddam and the allies could now only be settled by war. Every day the great voids of the Eastern Province of the kingdom were filling up with new deployments of troops. The first British troops had begun to appear: three hundred sappers from 39 Engineer regiment who were there to prepare the base camp of the Seventh Armoured Brigade – which at that stage was Britain's contribution to the land forces.

The regiment was normally based at Waterbeach in Cambridgeshire. The first few days in the one-hundred-degree heat had broiled most of their faces to a lobster pink. They were dossing down in a stuffy warehouse at the US base area at Jubail until they found a camp of their own. Their discomfort was intensified by the fact that they were required to wear fully laden webbing belts and carry their gas masks at all times. To combat the heat and the risk of dehydration, the sappers were advised to gulp down twenty-three pints of water a day.

It was clear almost from the outset that the initial British deployment would be reinforced. The Seventh Armoured Brigade, which had renamed itself the Desert Rats for the campaign, finally set up camp in the desert at the end of October. One day we went out to see them. It was a sight reminiscent of a hundred old Pathe newsreels as the sleek Challenger tanks of the Queen's Royal Irish Hussars bounded over the desert kicking up plumes of khaki dust. Their commander, Lt Col Arthur Denaro, watched with a delighted smile as the air filled with the powerful bass throb of Rolls-Royce engines. 'This really is cracking tank country,' he said.

The British with their heavy armour were slow to deploy. While the sappers were setting up a base area, the French Foreign Legion were already taking up their positions in the desert close to the frontier town of Hafer al Battin. The first elements arrived at mid-morning from the Red Sea port of Yanbu whence they had driven overland. The commander of the first unit to arrive, Lt Col Antoine Lecerf of the Second Foreign Infantry Regiment, surveyed the burning sands with barely supressed enjoyment.

'We shall put the swimming pool here, I think,' he said, pointing towards the wobbling heat of the horizon. 'I have brought my clubs with me. Perhaps you would care to join me for a game of golf later on.'

The French troops' relationship with their allies reflected their government's desire to contribute enough troops to be able to claim to be a significant element of the coalition, while retaining as much independence as possible. The 4,000 men and forty-eight light tanks and armoured vehicles deploying around Hafr al Battin were to remain outside the Allied Central Command structure and take their orders direct from General Roquejoffre in Riyadh. 'There's a problem with language,' claimed Lt Col Lecerf, with a broad grin. 'That's the only reason.' The Legion had forty nationalities represented in its ranks and less than forty per cent of the troops were French. Among the outsiders were a middle-class South African from a liberal Johannesburg family who had chosen the Legion rather than a university career, and who was frankly looking forward to the opportunity to kill someone, and a seasoned former Paratroop sergeant from Kent.

The French positions were close to the lines of the Arab troops who had been among the first to move into the desert at the start of the crisis. The most impressive were the Syrians who despatched 1,200 special forces to join the coalition. Syria had played a daring and clever game since the invasion. Before 2 August it had found itself in a difficult position in the region. The Soviet Union, its traditional sponsor and arms supplier, was pre-occupied with its own enormous problems and had let President Assad know that the relationship was henceforth to be strictly practical and that Damascus would be expected to pay for its arms bill.

At the same time Assad's long-time rival and arch enemy, Saddam Hussein, appeared to be succeeding in his ambition to place himself at the head of the Arab world. Assad's attempts to manoeuvre Syria closer to America and the West had been hampered by his record as a sponsor of international terrorist groups, and particularly Syria's involvement in an attempt to blow up an El Al airliner.

By unequivocally opposing the invasion and joining the allied military effort, Assad – whose regime was also supposedly based on Baathist principles – was placing himself and his country on the side of right and on the right side. As a proof of the earnestness of his intentions, the troops in the desert must have been among the best in the Syrian army. Many of them sported parachute wings and their demeanour was a far cry from the slouching, chain-smoking conscripts who used to be seen lounging at checkpoints in West Beirut. Their commander was General Deeb Mohammed Daher, a veteran of the 1973 fighting against Israel on the Golan Heights. Many of his men had fought against Israel in the Bekaa Valley nine years later during the invasion of Lebanon. When we met them one afternoon the general and his men had obviously prepared themselves for questions about the incongruity of anti-imperialist anti-Zionists joining forces with the United States. 'I am an Arab officer and I am ready to go and fight alongside another Arab army if it needs me,' said Gen. Daher.

The soldiers standing around in their skimpy fatigues had the same answer. 'The point is not whom we are fighting alongside,' said one, 'the point is that we are protecting the country from criminal action.'

A few miles down the road we ran into some of the remnants of Kuwait's 20,000-strong army who had managed to escape over the border. Their British-made Chieftain tanks sat in the sand with Kuwaiti pennants fluttering from the turrets, their guns pointed eagerly towards their homeland. The tanks showed little signs of engagement in battle. According to the accounts of the crews, however, they had all been in the thick of a desperate rearguard action. 'We fought until our ammunition ran out,' said a captain. 'The engines on these tanks are very bad, only 750-horsepower for a sixty-ton machine. If we had had Challengers the situation would have been very bad for them.' Behind the bravado one sensed a desperate desire to make amends. 'It won't be easy but there will be a victory – *inshallah*. And we will be the first into Kuwait. Our defence minister has told us we will be the first.'

Chapter Four

Returning to London for a break, I found that people seemed curiously resigned to the prospect of war. There was none of the soul-searching that had gone on during and after the Falklands. The justice of Kuwait's cause was everywhere accepted. On the Underground businessmen, secretaries and the teenagers with Sony Walkmans hissing in their ears wore 'Free Kuwait' badges. But the cause of Kuwait on its own was not enough to justify war, especially a war that promised chemical weapons on one side and devastating high-tech bombs on the other. Only the prospect of removing Saddam from the scene made the prospect worthwhile. The Hitler comparison had now become a stock rhetorical device, reached out for unthinkingly by allied politicians. For a few days at the beginning of November there was a brief flurry of expectation when it was thought that the allies might launch an early offensive, without waiting for further backing from the UN. The announcement of the extra 200,000 troops had been regarded in some quarters as a smokescreen intended to mask the intention of an early attack.

It was clear that nothing short of unconditional withdrawal would satisfy the main allies. On 18 November Saddam had announced that all the foreign hostages would be released, starting on Christmas Day. President Bush was unimpressed. If Saddam wanted to avoid war, he said, he must 'turn tail 180 degrees. There won't have to be a shot fired in anger if he does what he is supposed to do, which is comply fully with our conditions – the United Nations resolutions.'

In the meantime another UN resolution was in the making. Bringing careful but persistent pressure on the USSR, Bush and his Secretary of State James Baker had by the end of the month corralled enough support to land another diplomatic blow on Saddam. On 29 November the Security Council adopted Resolution 678 by twelve votes to two against (Cuba and Yemen), with China abstaining. The resolution re-affirmed the eleven previous resolutions relating to the crisis and noted that despite UN efforts Iraq still refused to withdraw from Kuwait 'in flagrant contempt of the council.' The UN, it went on, was prepared to allow Iraq 'one final opportunity, as a pause of goodwill' to comply with Resolution 660 and completely withdraw from Kuwait.

Unless it did so on or before 15 January, the second paragraph warned, member states were authorised 'to use all necessary means to uphold and implement Resolution 660 and all subsequent relevant resolutions and to restore international peace and security in the area.' This last phrase could surely have been taken by the allies as the authorisation to go beyond the mere liberation of Kuwait to carry out the other major war aim, the removal of Saddam.

Realistic hopes of any Arab diplomatic *démarche* succeeding had by now all but disappeared. King Hassan of Morocco had earlier called for an Arab summit to resolve the crisis. Iraq had supported the move but Egypt, Syria and Saudi Arabia immediately rejected it.

Towards the end of the month I returned to Amman. The prospect of a UN deadline was known by then. The realisation of the likelihood, if not the inevitability, of war had punctured the Jordanians' earlier pro-Saddam exuberance.

On Friday 23 November supporters of Iraq held a demonstration in the centre of Amman. Several thousand men gathered there to shout slogans against President Bush, President Mubarak, President Assad of Syria, against Israel and Margaret Thatcher. For some reason France seldom featured in the Arab demonstrators' hate-list, even though its colonialist activities in the area had been just as cynical and dishonest as those of the British. The range of the protestors' targets was a measure of Jordan's isolation. There was a feeling of nervousness in the air that had not been present two months before when the Imams were preaching Jihad and thousands were volunteering to fight alongside Saddam's troops. The tone of the preacher at the al Husseini mosque was imploring and moderate: American soldiers should leave Saudi Arabia and there should be a negotiated settlement of all the problems in the Middle East, he proposed. Even the demonstrators' banners had a respectful tone, with polite references to 'Mr Bush'. It was all very different from the bloodthirsty boasts of the fate awaiting the 'new crusaders' that had been blazoned across the banners in September.

The realisation was sinking in everywhere that Jordan had backed a loser. The Saudis had demonstrated that they were in no mood to be reasonable about Jordan's dilemma. They had expelled Jordanian diplomats, claiming they were spying, cut off oil supplies and blocked trade. This hostility of the Saudis towards King Hussein had its roots in the rivalry between the respective royal houses which had reached a climax when Ibn Saud defeated Sherif Hussein Ibn Ali, the Emir of Mecca, in 1924, driving the Hashemites out of the Hejaz and robbing them of their control of the Holy Places the following year.

The submerged hostility that still existed between the two clans surfaced in an extraordinary U.S. Intelligence document emanating from Saudi Arabia, which was circulated among American officials. Written early in November, it suggested that King Hussein had been plotting with Saddam before the invasion. The report was classified 'secret' and detailed the carving-up of the Arabian peninsula between them. It was entitled 'Saudi Suspicions of King Hussein: The Smoking Gun.'

It began: 'Since the inception of the Gulf Crisis the ruling al Saud have made no secret of their belief that King Hussein of Jordan (and President Ali Abdullah Salih of Yemen) were complicitous in a plot by Iraq's Saddam Hussein to partition the Kingdom of Saudi Arabia. They have alleged that Saddam promised King Hussein that his part of the booty would be Saudi Arabia's Western Province (the Hejaz) from which his great grandfather was driven by the founder of modern Saudi Arabia, King Fahd's father Abd al-Aziz (Ibn Saud).'

The report admitted that up until now there had been no specific evidence to back the charge. Instead the Saudis cited a number of circumstantial details, some of them admittedly curious. King Hussein had referred to himself in public as the 'Sharif', the Emir of Mecca's old title. At the same time Saddam had taken to referring to Saudi Arabia not by name but by its constituent parts: the Nejd, Hejaz and al Hasa. Another element was Hussein's apparent loyalty to Saddam, despite the fact that the latter represented everything that the King had historically abhorred.

But the report revealed a new development. Two weeks before the time of writing, it said, a trusted Western colleague with a reputation for prudence and probity, told the (US) ambassador that he had met a few days before with a senior member of the rich and influential Jeddah-based Alireza family. He had been informed by this individual, whom he declined to identify specifically, of an approach in June from Jordanian Crown Prince Hassan. It went on to state that Hassan had sought assistance in laying the basis for a restoration of Hashemite rule. The Alireza concerned had, by his own account, responded that no one in the Hejaz, which had prospered under the al Saud, was the least bit interested in seeing a return of the Hashemites to the region or in delinking the Hejaz from the oil wealth controlled by Riyadh.

To this Prince Hassan allegedly replied that one never knew what might happen and had urged his Alireza interlocutor to consider the matter. Prince Hassan had reportedly pressed the loyal Alireza on the matter again in July, only to be rebuffed once more.

The matter obviously interested the US ambassador as the report said he'd raised the story with the head of the Alireza clan, Sheikh Ahmed Alireza, who knew both King Hussein and Crown Prince Hassan and, the report speculated, who might have been the man the Crown Prince had approached.

The sheikh, it continued, 'winced visibly and displayed extreme discomfort.' With proper diplomatic sensitivity the ambassador 'immediately changed the subject.' Later, however, on the morning of 1 November, the ambassador heard an identical story from a member of the al Saud who was part of King Fahd's inner circle.

The report's anonymous author concluded: 'This story while second-hand has a concreteness lacking in earlier accounts of the Jordanian ruling family's alleged perfidy. Whether it is true or not, it is clearly believed by King Fahd and his immediate entourage and does much to explain the open animosity Fahd now displays toward King Hussein.'

To anyone who had ever seen Crown Prince Hassan the story seemed laughable. He was the quintessence of an Arab Occidentophile and the antithesis of the whispering conspirator. He was a high-minded idealist, portly and dignified, but markedly unregal, he had a pleasantly pompous view of the world and in his frequent meetings with journalists he expressed himself in the impenetrable language of the idealistic seminars that he loved to attend. He spoke of 'consequentalities' and 'modalities'. The idea of him proposing the restoration, sixty-five years on, of the Hashemites was absurd. On the other hand, in the Middle East widely believed conspiracy theories had taken root in much less promising soil than this.

While Jordan's intentions were being scrutinised with a hostile eye by East and West alike, its Syrian neighbour was receiving its reward for its prompt enrolment on the side of right. As early as 13 October, President Assad had felt

72

confident enough of his new respectability to launch an attack on General Michel Aoun, the leader of a section of the Maronite community in Lebanon, who had raised a rebellion against Syrian domination of his country in March the previous year. Aoun was an intensely irritating figure to Assad. Although he had quickly fallen from the high ideals with which he announced the start of his crusade, his continued defiance reminded the world of the extent of Syria's dominance in the affairs of its neighbour.

Until now, though, both the United States and Israel had made it clear that Assad would not be allowed to use decisive force to prise Aoun out of the presidential palace at Baabda in the hills above Beirut, where he had been holed up since taking on the presidency. That meant employing Syrian airpower. With the appearance of the Syrian Migs, Aoun's eighteen-month-long resistance crumbled immediately. He fled to the French Embassy for sanctuary and the Syrians moved in to extend their deployment into the Christian area.

By effectively allowing Assad a free hand against Aoun, the Americans and the West were essentially lending their tacit support to the traditional Syrian view that it had an overwhelming interest in Lebanon that necessitated controlling it as though it were a vassal state.

It was a big prize for Assad but his reward was not to end there. Late in November, David Gore-Booth, under secretary for the Middle East at the Foreign Office, made an unexpected visit to Damascus to meet the Foreign Minister Farouk al Sharaa for talks aimed at restoring the diplomatic relations which had been broken off four years before by Britain. Syria's deep involvement in the April 1986 Hindawi affair, when a thirty-two-year-old Jordanian, Nezar Hindawi, had used his pregnant Irish girlfriend as a dupe to try and plant a bomb on an El Al airliner at Heathrow, had exposed Damascus' rôle as a leading sponsor of international terror organisations. Later, Syrian complicity was suspected in the bombing of the Pan Am airliner which exploded over the Scottish town of Lockerbie in December 1988. For a long time the chief suspect for the latter atrocity was Ahmed Jibril, leader of the Popular Front for the Liberation of Palestine – General Command, which had its headquarters in Damascus.

Jibril was a cheery, leather-jacketed thug who looked more like a taxi driver than the revolutionary leader he claimed to be. With a little application it was always possible to meet him when in Damascus, a circumstance that was only possible because of the approval of the Syrian authorities. Jibril always denied involvement in the bombings, and was supported in this by the Syrian government. But he was happy to announce plans for the annihilation of the 'Zionist State' and over the years, scores – if not hundreds – of idealistic young men had been sent south from bases in Lebanon on suicidal missions against the Israeli forces. Their pictures were up on the walls of his office. One showed a group of smiling boys, no more than eighteen years old, in fatigues and *keffiyehs*, standing among the trees in a mountain-training camp in Lebanon. Their long hairstyles suggested the picture was taken about fifteen years before. It is highly unlikely that any of them is alive today.

There were offices of exiled Palestinian groups all over Damascus. The regular Popular Front for the Liberation of Palestine had its office there. So did the Democratic Front for the Liberation of Palestine. One was taken to see their leaders by courteous men who picked you up at the hotel. Etiquette demanded a long wait on arrival at the offices, usually a few spartan rooms, plastered with propaganda posters, in the basement of an apartment block – where bored bodyguards sat around smoking, and drinking constant cups of sweet tea. Then there would be the long, circumlocutory conversation; the hesitant, condition-laden replies before the polite inquiry as to what one personally thought of the situation. Exiled, with the prospect of that

74

exile stretching ahead endlessly, the Palestinians took a minute interest in Israeli affairs. They showed an intimate knowledge of the feuds, rivalries, deals and fixes that characterise Israeli politics. They hated the Israelis. But they were fascinated by them too. Like many outsiders they were prepared to accept Israel's carefully nurtured image of omnipotence against its enemies, which sits incongruously with its parallel claim to be under constant mortal threat from the surrounding Arabs.

Assad's hospitality to these groups was not idealistic. It was purely business, a means of exerting some influence over the PLO with whose leader, Yasser Arafat, he had maintained a long-standing enmity – culminating in his attempts to kill him during the siege of Tripoli in 1983. The international acceptance that Arafat had won through his strategy of moderation had significantly diminished Assad's ability to exercise control over Palestinian matters. Controlling the PLO had been a key aim of several leaders with ambitions of a dominating regional rôle, and one pursued in the preceding year by Saddam.

But now Arafat's reputation was in tatters and Syria was about to take a step further towards the warm light of international recognition. On 28 November the British foreign secretary, Douglas Hurd, announced that diplomatic relations with Damascus had been restored. In doing so he added: 'We have received from the Syrian government assurances that Syria will continue its strenuous efforts to obtain the release of Western hostages in Lebanon and confirmation that Syria rejects acts of international terrorism, and will take action against the perpetrators of such acts which are supported by convincing evidence.' He also made a mysterious reference to having received a 'confidential account' of the Syrian position on the Israeli bombing attempt – an incident in which a British court had established that the Syrian Embassy in London was involved up to its neck.

The references to hostages and terrorists were the necessary fig leaves to a *realpolitik* decision. Syria had repeatedly said it would do its utmost to free the hostages. Despite its control of the southern suburbs of Beirut and the town of Baalbek where the kidnappers lurked, they had produced few results.

It was generally agreed that Iranian, rather than Syrian, influence was the crucial element in bringing about releases, although the practice of handing the hostages over to their ambassadors in Damascus, rather than Beirut, allowed Syria to gain undeserved kudos. The assurances on terrorism did not constitute any concession on the part of Assad. He had said on several occasions that he would take action against anyone guilty of terrorist offences living in Syrian territory – if that guilt could be proved. As it was, Syria was in the best position to supply the evidence. There was no indication that it was going to do that. Syria's rehabilitation did not much interest the outside world. But to anyone with an interest in the region it was proof that George Bush's crusade was as tarnished as any other imperialist adventure.

CHAPTER FIVE

The plane I took back to Saudi from Paris a few days before Christmas 1990 was full of desperate men trying to soak up as much drink as possible before dipping into the alcohol-free airspace of the kingdom. Among them was a small, wiry figure in a blue knitted cap and smudged tattoos. Billy was drunk. He looked as if he had escaped from a Bruce Springsteen song about pain, patriotism and Vietnam. 'I love Texas and I love my country,' he burbled, calling to the snooty Air France stewardess for yet another glass of champagne. 'Friend, I love my President and I'm ready to die for my country. I was in Vietnam when I was eighteen. I got wounded three times there. Well, now I got the call from the Department of Defense, but I don't rightly know what I'll be doing.' He drained the plastic cup, doused his Philip Morris in the dregs of the champagne and began crooning the old 'Country Joe and the Fish' anti-war anthem: *And it's one two three, what are we fighting for?* The next line, of course, is, *Don't ask me, I don't give a damn.* Billy, who declined to reveal the precise circumstances in which he was serving in Saudi Arabia, may have been happy to have been back in the thick of things, but many of the 300,000 American and other troops now in the country were much more cautious about the coming war.

A few days later I was in the al Shula shopping centre in al Khobar when I ran into a disconsolate trio of US servicemen looking at the electronic goodies in an Asian hi-fi and camera store before going off to get a fake McDonalds' hamburger and a near beer.

Like many of their age, they had joined up in response to the distinctly unmilitaristic message of the Eighties' recruiting ads which urged 'Be All You Can Be' and showed earnest bespectacled soldiers seated behind computer screens. The prevailing ethos was Beetle Bailey, rather than Rambo. The three were army helicopter technicians and had been working at the Dhahran airbase since early in the crisis. 'We want to go home and see our families,' said Rocky, a pleasant twenty-one-year-old from upstate New York. 'Living in a tent ain't so hot.'

Will, the same age and wearing an alarming Mohican haircut, was bored. 'Worrying about the deadline helps, but if nothing happens . . . not knowing when you're going home. That's the hardest part.'

Military psychologists agreed that the existence of the 15 January 1991 deadline had probably reinforced morale. Until it was reached there was a sense of expectation that kept the Saudi blues at bay. The military authorities had been keeping a close eye on the mental health of the troops. They had employed a screening process before deployment, weeding out the obviously unstable. At headquarters in Riyadh the US air force had set up a stress-management centre to advise officers and men on how to spot danger signs among their comrades and what action to take. The plan was for sufferers to be counselled initially by their buddies. Only if that failed were the professionals to be brought in. The unit also promoted 'unit bonding', which in earlier times was called camaraderie. All the studies had shown that the more 'bonding' there was, the fewer casualties. But apart from a few cases of desperate soldiers swigging methanol to get high – risking blindness, brain damage and death in the process – there had been little for the mental-health officers to do.

The arrival of Christmas saw a flurry of visits by allied dignitaries. The British sent Prince Charles. The Saturday before Christmas Day he turned up riding on a tank for the TV cameras at the camp of Colonel Arthur Denaro's Queen's

Royal Irish Hussars. He seemed strangely ill at ease and bad-tempered as he inspected the tank crews. Seeing the media, he looked surprised. 'What the bloody hell are you doing here?' he asked in mock anger. 'Keeping you in a job,' a photographer muttered under his breath.

He looked more comfortable the following day when he visited the Dhahran airbase. Among the objects deemed suitable for his inspection was something after his own heart. It was a low-risc, low cost vernacular building, constructed from local materials, in which people could come together as a community. The bomb shelter under construction by the men of 53 Field Squadron 39 Engineering Regiment was a thing of primitive beauty, reminiscent of the lower storeys of the Ziggurat of Ur. Its creators took a fierce pride in their work. 'It's the state-of-the-art shelter in Saudi Arabia,' said Staff Sgt Mick Blomquist. 'We lay the sandbags as if they were bricks. The Americans just throw them one on top of the other. There's no method in their madness so they just fall over.' The shelter required 10,000 individually filled sandbags. And the sandbag, according to Warrant Officer Carl Holman, another member of the team, was a key element in the success of the construction.

Here the British again had a lead over the Americans because of their insistence on sticking to traditional technology. He waved a small, green hessian sack. 'It's got binding power,' Holman declared, 'not like this.' He pointed to an inferior-looking khaki plastic bag of the type favoured by the Americans and the Saudis. 'The American designers have got to go back to natural fibres.'

On Christmas Day itself there were some half-hearted attempts to celebrate with a Santa doing the rounds of the British positions by helicopter. Well-wishers had donated gift parcels to the men and unscrupulous retailers had emptied their warehouses of superannuated stock in a self-serving patriotic gesture. Some of the gifts went down better than others. Cigarettes, sweets and phone cards were popular.

Cassettes of elderly minor pop stars who had fallen into obscurity before many of the soldiers were walking, were not. The troops wrapped tinsel round their gun barrels and the communications antennae, and dressed up in silly clothes. Amid the innocent raucousness of the festivities, more like an overgrown children's party than an adult celebration, the thought of the coming confrontation was never far away. 'I'll lose a lot of friends if the fighting starts,' said Private John Ritchie, a nineteen-year-old from Aberdeen.

On Christmas Day, President Bush had broadcast a message to the troops on the Armed Forces Radio. He told them, 'We are in the Gulf because the free world must not reward aggression, because of our vital interests and because of the brutality and danger of Saddam Hussein.' Now Billy would know what he was fighting for.

According to the American briefers in Riyadh, the Iraqis were continuing to improve an array of fortifications that now spread the length of the Kuwaiti coast and cut through the desert in an arc to shield Kuwait City. The coastal defences consisted of barbed wire, well-placed mortars and anti-aircraft guns, minefields, barriers and trenches. Inland, lay a daunting band of fortifications. A typical cross-section, they said, consisted of trenches, minefields, anti-tank and personnel barriers. In some places they had prepared pits full of oil that would be ignited when the offensive came. Once through these defences, the attackers would face concentrated artillery fire from the Iraqi gunlines.

By the end of December, the Americans claimed Iraq had more than half a million troops in the theatre, with 4,000 tanks, 2,500 armoured personnel carriers and 2,700 artillery pieces in and around Kuwait. The figures had remained remarkably constant considering the briefers reported with monotonous regularity that Saddam was 'continuing to pour troops into the area.' One day at the end of December we drove up to Khafji and persuaded a Saudi coastguard officer to take us to their most forward positions. From a Beau

Geste style fort on the coast we could clearly see the Iraqi defences. Along the beach on the other side of no man's land 200 metres away, the sand had been bulldozed into foxholes. The lorries which at first sight we had taken for normal civilian trucks, turned out to be painted in green-and-sand camouflage when viewed through German artillery spotters' glasses. 'Last night I saw a lot of traffic coming in, tanks and trucks,' said our guide, Lieutenant Awad. 'We could see them through the night vision glasses. There are more of them here now than there ever were before.'

Every day the two sides observed each other through their binoculars, the Saudis from their romantically castellated fort, the Iraqis from among the palm trees of the holiday-brochure beach. Did they ever wave at each other? 'We are enemies now,' said Lieutenant Awad. 'The only thing I would wave at them would be a gun.' As we left we had a frosty conversation with a detachment of US Navy Seals, the special forces unit, who had a camp by the fort. Further into the dunes a British Special Forces unit had set up a radar dome.

If the Iraqis were reinforcing, so too were the allies but on an infinitely greater scale. At times the road from Dhahran to the Kuwaiti border seemed like a continuous Moscow Mayday parade as tanks, APCs and support vehicles rolled north under the cold, blue sky. Every twenty-four hours, according to American figures, 3,500 trucks were cruising the highways.

We passed a dismal 1990 New Year's Eve in an Indian restaurant in al Khobar. We were the only people in the place and the waiters wanted to go home early. We were all in bed by eleven o'clock. The previous New Year's Eve I had spent in Bucharest. The one before in Jerusalem. Two years before that it had been Basra. The Iran–Iraq war was still going on then, and the Iraqis had taken a party of journalists to the front line to witness some meaningless 'victory'. At that time the war had long settled into a stalemate – with each side launching alternate attacks during the winter campaigning season when the more temperate climate made fighting easier. The rest of the time they harassed each other with artillery fire. Life for the troops was not too bad. They were rotated frequently and were reasonably well looked after. They turned their bunkers and dugouts into homes, with couches, radios and even TV sets.

On that New Year's Eve in Basra, I'd gone with some colleagues to one of the many nightclubs. In the pre-war days they had been patronised by merchant seamen from cargo ships docking at the busy port, but at this time the clientele were off-duty soldiers enjoying some R and R. The club was the size of a hangar and it was packed. The tables were loaded with beer and half-bottles of Johnny Walker Black Label, the Iraqis' favourite bevvy. Five plump whores were doing a brisk trade by the bar. They seemed to be able to turn around their clients in less than five minutes, always reappearing looking cheerful and fresh without a lacquered hair out of place. The soldiers were boisterous and friendly, and flirtatious with the women in the company. At midnight the floor show stopped. Everyone stood up. From the loudspeaker came blaring the tune of 'Happy Birthday to You'.

It was hard to associate those amiable men with the murderous deeds now being done in Kuwait.

The day before the 1991 New Year dawned there had been a strong signal of American intentions from Vice President Dan Quayle. In a visit to the troops he said that President Bush had been 'patient enough' in waiting for a peaceful solution and he criticised members of Congress who said more time should be given for the UN blockade of Iraq to work. There was now a new urgency among the journalists as they underwent their Nuclear Biological and Chemical training, struggling in and out of the cumbersome masks and stifling, charcoal-impregnated suits. The American mask was a design nightmare which came complete with a sinister plastic hood that deepened the science-fiction monster effect.

The JIB began deciding who would get a place on the 'pools', the small teams of correspondents who would be authorised to cover the fighting at the fronts. The networks, the major American newspapers, groups and news agencies were automatically included. But the JIB had left only two places for 'international' reporters and, as a courtesy to their hosts, a further two for the Saudi press. The JIB director had made it clear he would prefer that the places were taken by 'Brits'. Charles Richards of the *Independent* was chosen to go with the army and I was selected for the Marines pool.

On 8 January we went out for a trial run in the field. We spent the morning watching Marines firing mortars at piles of tyres and missing more often than they hit. More successful was a co-ordination exercise between forward air-controllers and Marine AV 8Bs, the American version of the Harrier. From one of the air-controllers I heard the stock justification for the war that was to be repeated to me innumerable times thereafter whenever a political discussion arose.

'As far as I can see there are two options,' said Captain Vinnie Savoia. 'Saddam can stay in Kuwait and lose his whole army. Or he can pull out, and I'll have to come back here in two years' time.'

We spent the night at the base of a reserve tank regiment. As we approached we saw the armour rolling back for the night after a day of exercises. They came out of the setting sun in line astern. For a few moments the twilight flooding through the dust clouds and bathing the rounded hulls of the M60s created an epic, Turneresque scene. As the tanks throbbed and jangled past, their names could be seen freshly stencilled on the barrels: *Grim Reaper. Hell Raiser. Public Enemy.* American troops seemed particularly drawn to portraying themselves as villains capable of any sort of excess and outrage. They would announce on their helmets and vehicles that they were 'born to kill', or whatever. The soldiers with the most bloodcurdling messages were usually the baby-faced ones, who seemed to be trying to convince both themselves and those around them that they were up to the work ahead.

In the camp that night there was little macho talk. The reservists were a mixed and mostly well-educated crew. A month before they had been studying for exams, selling insurance or serving behind counters. Serving in the reserves means soldiering at weekends and going away to camp for two weeks in the summer. For many it is a way of paying their way through college or supplementing their income. For veterans it was means of staying in touch with the Corps.

That night after chow, as the stars asserted themselves in the black canopy of the desert sky in great glittering bands, I stood in the freezing sand talking with a young sergeant called Davis. He was twenty-three years old and had been finishing his law degree in North Carolina when the crisis intervened. He hoped to become a district attorney, 'And when I'm dreaming maybe a judge.' He had old-fashioned views about legal ethics. 'The idea of lawyers advertising sticks in my craw.' Indeed he was pleasantly old-fashioned about almost everything. He had been to one concert in his life. It was Frank Sinatra and his girlfriend had bought the tickets. He took a simple view of the justice of the cause. Kuwait had been invaded and the wrong had to be redressed.

Other Marines, even the outwardly cynical, seemed to have taken to heart the commander-in-chief's rhetoric about the changes blowing through the world. 'I really think Bush believes this new-world-order bullshit,' a hard-bitten sergeant told me approvingly. 'We've been the guys in white hats standing around on the sidelines for too long. It's time to control the guys in black hats. I believe that in twenty years' time when the Russians have sorted out their problems we'll be policing the world together.'

To almost every soldier I spoke to that day, war had now become desirable. At one level it was a simple fatalistic desire to get on with it and get it over with, the quicker to get home. At another, war, a decisive war, was necessary to give their experience a value. At some point during the run-up to a war,

The Protagonists

Saddam Hussein (previous page), Norman Schwarzkopf *and* Sir Peter de la Billière

War at night. A Patriot missile is launched in defence of Tel Aviv *and* anti-aircraft fire flares over Baghdad (opposite)

War on the ground

The
liberation
of
Kuwait

Famous Victory?
Kurdish refugees

the survival instinct is overtaken by the desire for some crucial adventure that will imbue life with a new meaning. Even level-headed Sgt Davis spoke of the necessity to have 'one adventure in your life, something to tell the younger ones – like the Non Comms here go on about Vietnam.'

For these reasons there was a feeling of dissatisfaction at the prospect of a diplomatic settlement. For the crisis to end in a whimper, now, would mean another one later that would end with a nuclear bang. In the event, the last hope of a negotiated settlement ended with the talks in January between Secretary of State Baker and the Iraqi foreign minister Tariq Aziz in Geneva. For a time it seemed that the discussions were going rather well after the meeting ran on for several hours beyond its allotted time. Down at the JIB the mood of the journalists lightened as the minutes ticked past. At lunchtime there was a report that 'substantial' progress had been made. I passed on the news to a gung ho US army colonel, a public-relations warrior. His face turned sour. 'Shit!' he said. 'That bastard Saddam.'

A few hours later the colonel could relax again. Baker emerged from the meeting to declare that he had 'heard nothing today . . . that suggested to me any flexibility whatsoever in complying with the UN Security council resolutions.'

In the *Arab Times*, the Saudi English language newspaper, the approach of 'K Day' was marked each day with a calendar – sometimes accompanied by an infantile poem. In the Eastern Province the expatriates were drifting away. Since the previous weekend the British Embassy in Riyadh and the Consulate in al Khobar had been distributing gas masks. Signs appeared in the hotels directing guests to the basements normally only seen by the waiters and laundry workers, but which would now serve as underground shelters. The expatriates who decided to stay were constructing their own, laying in supplies of water, taping over windows and doors to seal the chosen room from gas. In the Eastern Province all but 1,000 of the 4,000 Britons had left.

British Airways laid on extra flights and promised to keep services running until the eve of 'K Day'. France, Germany and Spain ordered their nationals and their families out of the kingdom. Surprisingly the Americans, usually sensitive to the point of being alarmist about the safety of their citizens, showed remarkable sang-froid. No move was made to order out the 20,000 us citizens in the country. Nor were they issued with gas masks. 'We are not convinced that there is a need for them,' said the official spokesman. One explanation for this coolness was an anxiety to avoid disconcerting their Saudi hosts by any action that might create panic among the local population.

For the long-suffering and usually disregarded army of third-world expatriate workers, the situation was more complicated. Most were stoically resigned to staying, reasoning that if they left they might not be able to get back in again and their families would lose a precious source of income. Even if they wanted to go, their governments were not happy to have them back. India, with 600,000 nationals in Saudi Arabia, the Philippines with 400,000 and Sri Lanka with 100,000: all advised their countrymen to stay put, fearing the strain on their economies from a flood of returnees.

The weekend before the deadline several Arab leaders appealed to Baghdad to see sense. Leading the chorus was Hafez al Assad, who implored Saddam to take 'the courageous step' of leaving Kuwait and averting a war. He also made an unprecedented broadcast to Baghdad, pledging that if Iraq was attacked after it withdrew, 'Syria with all its potentials, materially and morally, will stand beside Iraq in one trench, fighting with it strongly until victory is achieved.'

With the departure of Perez de Cuellar, empty-handed, from Baghdad on the eve of the deadline, even the most desperate optimists gave up hope of peace. That night I was contacted by an officer from the JIB and told to attend at five the following morning. I was going to the desert to live with the Marines.

CHAPTER SIX

Our base was to be a massive logistics complex still being constructed in the middle of the desert about fifty kilometres south-west of Khafji. The base lay on one side of the Main Supply Route: a swathe of flattened sand running inland from the coast across Northern Saudi Arabia that connected up all the elements strung along the front line. It had been raining for thirty-six hours straight and the sun and wind were only beginning to dry the place out. Normally Saudi Arabian rain amounted to little more than a perfume spray of moisture that wetted the desert for a few days every year. The rain that fell on the kingdom between 13 January and 15 January 1991 was European stair-rods – delivering, it was said, two-thirds of the average annual precipitation in a few short hours. It seemed another indication of the extent to which the times were out of kilter. All the tents and Porta-kabins had been sunk into the ground to protect against air attack. As a result the water had coursed down the sand walls covering the floors of the bunkers with sludge. All over the base, gangs of Marines were filling sandbags from the dryer patches of ground and laying them in carpets over the lakes at the bottom of their workshops, stores and 'hootches'. The HQ stretched over 100 square kilometres, and was designed to supply the needs of an American army fighting a European war against the Soviets. It was a massive storehouse of ammunition, fuel, water, food and medical supplies spread out to limit damage in the increasingly unlikely event of an air attack and further protected by sand walls or as we came to call them, using the Arabic name, *berms*.

The stocks were monitored from a computer centre. When hostilities began, the Direct Support Groups further up the line would move the supplies to Mobile Combat Service Detachments who would ferry them to the fighting troops. The idea was that the four journalists attached to the base would move around the front with the combat service detachments, following the progress of the battle.

The base had only been under construction for ten days but according to its commander, Brigadier General Chuck Krulak, it was already capable of carrying out its basic function. Gen. Krulak had worked in the White House and was PR conscious. His father had been a famous Marine. He was short, wiry and energetic with chiselled Dick Tracy features. Every night he joined the chow-line along with his men and went to the church tent on Sunday. Under his direction the business of completing the building, and the stocking of the base, crowded out any consideration of what was happening elsewhere.

On my first morning at the base I came across a Marine company standing-to outside their tents in the chilly morning air while the sergeant gave them a pep talk. 'I don't know anyone who doesn't want to go home,' he said. 'You're not the only ones living in holes because we all are. We're tired and dirty and we stink, but that's life in the magic kingdom.'

Life on the base seemed to be just as tedious as at any military establishment, despite the expectation of action. The Marines rose as dawn broke at about five-thirty and trudged through the sand to the mess hall where they queued up for platefuls of eggs, bacon, sausages, waffles and maple syrup. Then work began and continued through the day, breaking at lunchtime for an MRE. Meals Ready to Eat were the latest refinement in military catering. They came in thick brown plastic sacks that required Boot Camp training to tear

88

open. According to their manufacturers they could be stored for years and remain edible, or at least not poisonous. Some of them had the date of manufacture stamp on the side. Thus, opening one was rather like opening one of the time capsules that are sometimes buried in the foundations of new buildings, containing articles that are imagined to represent the *Zeitgeist*. In a way that is what the MRES were. The main courses included corned-beef hash, meatballs in tomato sauce and chilli, as if some equal-opportunity law necessitated the inclusion of representative dishes of the main ethnic groups. There were crackers and sachets of peanut butter and apple jelly to spread on them. Another little pack contained toothpicks, a miniature bottle of tabasco and chewing gum. But unlike the ration packs of the Vietnam era there were no cigarettes. Indeed only a minority of the soldiers smoked. Chewing tobacco was something else. Many of the white Marines were country boys from the South where the practice was still strong. It was, anyway, a Marine tradition, endorsed by the Marine commandant himself. The tobacco was dark, moist and scented. You didn't chew it as much as suck it, placing a thick wad between front teeth and lower lip and letting it sit there until a sort of cud had formed. Occasionally the surplus spit would be delicately expelled in a carefully aimed yellow jet.

At nightfall the Marines would return to the mess hall for another huge meal. Then they would go back to their hootches and prepare for bed.

The days could be hot. But once the sun sank quickly in a spectacular orange ball behind the dunes, the cold soon gripped the sand. After dark the camp was deserted and the showing of lights was forbidden even though the nearest enemy position was at least sixty kilometres away. Inside the hootches, those with electricity sat and played cards and listened to their boom boxes. The blacks played rap. The whites, Country and Western and Heavy Metal. In some units there was a half-hearted attempt to recreate the atmosphere of Vietnam by playing Jimi Hendrix and The Doors. In the tents without power, once the light went there was nothing to do but sleep.

The night of 16 to 17 January I woke up several times because of the cold. Each time I could hear the sound of aircraft flying high overhead. I awoke again properly at six. Lieutenant Pat Gibbons was listening to the BBC news. 'They've bombed Baghdad,' he said. We stumbled out of the tent and looked up. The planes were coming over in v formation, like black daggers moving across the sky. You could see the ordnance hanging heavy under the wings. Barely had the rumble from one wave passed than the air was filled with the noise of another. Occasionally a distant hollow thump announced that a bomb had landed. Small groups gathered around radios to hear the ABC Nightline TV news being relayed on the forces network. Their defence expert was eulogising the rôle of the Tomahawk cruise missile, scores of which had been fired from the US fleet in the Gulf. There was an appreciative laugh when he claimed it could be launched in Boston and it would land between the goalposts of the Washington Redskins. This, it turned out, was a perfectly accurate boast.

All round the camp, there was a sense of excitement and satisfaction. The waves of aircraft overhead gave one a warm sense of reassurance and conviction as to the inevitability of an allied victory. A major, impatient with excitement, had climbed up on a berm as if the extra metre or so of elevation would enable him to peer into the destruction that was taking place over the horizon. 'So far so good,' he said. 'If they follow the classic approach they'll bomb for a few weeks. Then it depends on if he capitulates or not, whether we send land forces.' The sight of the jets had brought the prospect of going home nearer, raised the hope in some quarters that the soldiers might not have to fight at all. They gave off an aura of destructiveness that was immensely comforting to ground forces who had been living with the fear of a long drawn-out and bloody slog in the sand. 'If they bomb for a couple of weeks then there will be nothing left,' said a young sergeant, scarcely bothering to hide the relief in his voice. Nobody seemed to want to work up much sympathy for the Iraqis on the receiving end.

'I can't say I feel sorry for them,' said Ron Schaffer, a twenty-nine-year-old sergeant from Norfolk Virginia. 'They live in their country and they have to follow their leader like we follow our President. They're doing what they have to do and we're doing what we have to do.' He paused to think about conditions on the other side. 'There will be massive confusion. They thought they were prepared for what was to come. But everyone who fights Mike Tyson plans beforehand that they will get hit. Then the plan goes haywire because they didn't know how hard the punch was going to be.'

There was no sign that the launching of the attack had provoked a serious response from the Iraqis, though there were sketchy reports that a few shells had landed around Marine positions nearer the border.

The great fear was that Saddam would reply immediately by launching missiles with chemical warheads. The threat from chemical weapons was stressed constantly in all the Western armies of the allies, even though the commanders knew the real risk was small. Gas masks had to be carried everywhere and decontamination drills were regularly practised.

The morning after the launching of the air-war, we were awakened by the single, long drawn-out note of a siren, warning that a chemical attack had taken place or was just about to. Suddenly the scenario painted in lurid colours by the Nuclear Biological and Chemical warfare instructors seemed about to become reality. Inside the tent there was just enough light to find our canvas gas-mask bags and pull out the clumsy apparatus with its sinister green plastic hood. As soon as we had got them on loudspeakers around the camp announced we were at 'MOPP Level Four'. In the acronym-speak beloved of the Western militaries, 'MOPP'

91

stood for 'Mission Oriented Protective Posture' and four was the highest level, requiring troops to put on charcoal-impregnated trousers and smocks, rubber overshoes and gloves. The design of the American NBC was shoddy and thoughtless. The trousers of the medium-size suit would fit a baby elephant and the waistband soon slipped down around my knees. The boots were clumsy and shapeless, laborious to lace up and full of crevices and folds where chemicals could collect.

We listened to the news. During the early morning Saddam had launched Scud attacks on Israel and Dhahran. Eventually, an hour and a quarter later, the all-clear was sounded and everyone thankfully tore off the suits. They were stiflingly hot and the mask induced claustrophobia. Worst of all it amplified the sound of your breathing, reminding you how easy it would be for it to stop.

The reason for the alarm was never made clear. One version was that the alert had been sounded when a Marine thought he heard the warning noise from a chemical detection device and fired off a red-and-green cluster flare, signifying a possible chemical attack. Thereafter false alarms became commonplace, but until the end they were always taken seriously.

As the days went by the sound of war drifted closer to the camp. The distant banging and thumping had an elemental quality, so that after a while it became almost normal, part of the topographical and climactic features of our surroundings. The bad weather continued: cloud, rain and mist. The Iraqi conscripts, crouching in their foxholes, must have been praying for it to last. The cloud hid them from their hunters and fewer missions were being flown, providing a little respite from the endless bombardments. The Americans were equally fervent in urging the elements to lift, so that the timetables of destruction could be met.

The weird weather was producing weird effects. One

morning dawn broke brightly enough but two hours later the sky suddenly darkened and within minutes was almost black, with the rising wind adding an extra Macbethian air of menace. After twenty more minutes the normal grey had returned, mocking the advertisements in the military papers which urged the folks at home to send sunblock 'to shield your loved one from the hot desert sun.' Overnight, patches of vivid green appeared in the sands, the shoots of some optimistic and irrepressible desert weed, and small black-and-white birds darted over the ground.

Near our camp they were preparing a holding pen for Iraqi prisoners, a large square of sand fenced off with razor wire and with a watchtower at each corner. It was a highly literal structure. Empty though it was, one could already imagine the herds of disconsolate prisoners shuffling around inside the perimeter and the bored guards looking down, indifferent, chewing their tobacco, resting on their machine guns.

A few days later we saw some real prisoners. We had been taken to visit a Marine camp near the border town of Khafji when a lance corporal took advantage of the absence of any superiors to whisper to us, 'Look over there.' In the distance at the far side of the base we saw a group of dark-skinned men in dark-green uniforms being led across the sand. After much cajoling we were allowed to go and have a closer look. The twelve men were, it seemed, the first Iraqis to have been captured in the war. They'd been manning anti-aircraft batteries and shoulder-held surface-to-air missiles on nine Kuwaiti oil-platforms in the Gulf when they were captured the night before by a joint force from the guided missile frigate USS *Nicholas* and a Kuwaiti patrol boat, supported by helicopter gunships. About five of their comrades had been killed and another four wounded in the incident. By coincidence I was to meet one of the wounded five months later in his home in Basra.

The Iraqis had clearly put up a good fight but there was no defiance left now. They sat crouched in a hole in the sand, barefoot, cross-legged and unshaven. They looked like all the beaten in war: numbed, slow, biddable. They were youngish and badly dressed with navy sweaters over their skimpy olive fatigues. Every one had a moustache. Marine NCOs moved among them, handing out MRE packs. Some were too far gone to manage to eat and the Americans knelt down beside them to help spoon down the food. The captors were solicitous and moved gently as if dealing with overgrown and rather slow schoolchildren. As one captive was led down to the pit, a black NCO put his arm around his shoulder. Elsewhere a slightly injured Iraqi sat hunched and dazed while a soldier examined his foot.

The Americans would allow the Reuter photographer in our group, Charles Platiau, to film only the backs of the Iraqis as they were 'not exhibits in a zoo'. Supervising events was a tall, Marine security officer who declined to identify himself. He was gaunt and bespectacled, looks that gave him – misleadingly as it turned out – the appearance of a cinema psychopath. He was anxious to let us know that the men would be treated well. 'Thumbscrews and racks are a thing of the past,' he said. 'You can break anybody and get them to say whatever you want to hear. But you get a better response if you treat them humanely. We found that in Vietnam.'

When mealtime was ended they were to be taken away for interrogation to discover their names and ranks, given a medical check-up, boots, sleeping bags and gas masks. 'There are mosques around here and they have been told that when they hear the call to prayer they can exercise the religious moves accordingly,' said the gaunt Intelligence officer. As we left it was beginning to get dark and a few heavy drops of rain were starting to fall. Up the road the prisoners' comrades were preparing for the inevitable night of earth-shaking bombardment that lay ahead.

The following day we were taken to see some Marine helicopter pilots at a small airbase at al Mishab, on the Gulf coast near the Kuwaiti border. Their manner, their looks,

94

their radiant health and energy could not have been a greater contrast to the condition of the wretched Iraqis. They were sitting around in their overalls, awaiting the order to climb into their Cobra helicopter gunships and take off. They answered questions thoughtfully, politely and fully, expensive dentistry ·flashing from suntanned faces, eyes hidden behind Ray Bans. A few, like the Iraqis, had moustaches. But these additions were lifestyle statements, hinting at Californian beaches and open-topped cars, a world away from the frightened conformity of the inhabitants of the bunkers they were blasting every day.

They had been in action from the beginning of the air-war, attacking suspected Iraqi positions just over the border from Khafji. A thirty-ish captain from Texas described attacking his first target: 'a small building on the coast, probably someone's vacation condo down on the beach.

'We just ran up on it and hit it with a TOW missile, rockets and some 20mm cannon. We were getting a little return fire from small arms and something that might have been an anti-tank missile.' But after pounding the emplacement for five minutes any resistance had ended. The captain had not had time to be frightened, 'But it made me more apprehensive about running on the next target.'

In fact on the next sortie, against a sandbagged building near the coast, there was no return fire at all. Several of the pilots said they had faced little or no threat from anti-aircraft artillery. 'We're surprised at how sparsely they're spread out in Southern Kuwait,' said the captain. 'We were anticipating a thick band of frontier defences.'

It was natural to think at this stage that the feebleness of the Iraqi responses was deliberate. That they were holding back, lulling the allies into a false move, later to unleash the firepower we had heard so much about from the American Intelligence reports, to maximum effect.

To date the only sign that an enemy existed was the sporadic nightly bombardments mounted by Iraqi gunners from across the borders. These were unspectacular affairs: the odd salvo of artillery, the occasional FROG missile. The shots appeared to be aimed at random, but such was the density of allied troops in that corner of the border zone that they inevitably landed near some position or other, and several soldiers were lightly wounded by shell splinters. Despite strenuous efforts by the American Special Forces who crossed the border to silence them, the Iraqis managed to fire off a few rounds after dusk fell. They were gestures of defiance rather than part of any serious military operations.

Nonetheless, for the great majority of the Marines, it was the closest they had come to the experience of combat. After meeting the helicopter pilots we spent the night in a nearby Marine base where a few of the Iraqi shells had landed. As the men stood around digesting the evening chow, they could talk of little else. A group were taking bets on what time they would hear the first explosion. Earlier, inside the mess hall, someone had passed round a jagged piece of rocket casing, probably from a Soviet-made FROG, telling everyone that he was going to exhibit it in the personal war museum he was already planning when he got home.

The inexperience of the Marines was both touching and alarming. If they were going to get this excited over a few haphazardly lobbed shells, how would they react to a proper bombardment? To what extent was the Corps' intense self-regard justified? The Marines certainly had a high opinion of their own abilities, comfortably up there with the extravagant *amour-propre* of the British Paras and the French Foreign Legion. Even the lowliest clerk, whose duties were as far removed from martial glamour as possible, invested his activities with a fierce pride. 'What does it mean to be a Marine, sir? To be the best there is.' This was the response from storeman to fighter pilot. The Corps ethos was complicated. In one form it was an attempt to combine the worlds of Ancient Sparta and *Marvel* Comics, implying superhuman abilities in the fields of endurance and destruction. This was echoed in their durable nick-name for themselves, 'Devil Dogs', a term that dated from the First World War and which was heard more often than the Vietnam-era 'Grunt', with its overtones of self-disparagement. The idea of absolute negation of the individual will was suggested in the brutal 'zero to three' haircuts which almost everybody wore, whereby the victim's head is shaved up the sides leaving a small patch of hair on top, not so dissimilar to the styles adopted by medieval knights to cushion the weight of their helmets.

But into this carefully constructed military sub-society, America kept breaking in. Asked by the Marine newspaper, *Brown Side Out*, about his wife's reaction to the news that he was going to Saudi Arabia, Corporal Charles K. Piceno, twenty-three, replied solemnly that, 'She went through a process of denial, rejection and withdrawal as many wives do.' This psycho-babble tripped lightly off many lips, reminding you that these disciplined, polite, motivated young men were the children of the shopping mall. More and more, one came to ponder Saddam's brutal prediction to the American ambassador in Baghdad, April Glaspie: 'Yours is a society that cannot accept 10,000 dead in one battle.'

The men fighting in the Gulf were older than those who had gone before them to Vietnam, and more literate. 'Our average reading was a comic-book,' said a former Marine and Vietnam veteran in our pool. 'That was about the level. The average age of a field unit in Vietnam was about nineteen and a half. We had a guy with us who was twenty-four and we called him "Pops".'

But the key social difference from the Vietnam era was the presence of sizeable numbers of women. The 130 at the base made up eight per cent of the personnel. You saw them everywhere: standing guard duty; seated behind communications consoles; even resignedly doing their share of the worst job imaginable, burning the latrine pits, the 'shitters'. They had become an unremarkable feature of everyday life.

The need for massive logistics bases close to the front line had pushed more women soldiers, mostly employed in rear-echelon duties, closer to the fighting than ever before. It was a development that they viewed with mixed emotions.

'I don't feel women should be up here unless their job calls for it,' Corporal Patricia Perez, a dark attractive woman from New York State told me as she took a break from digging a trench. She worked for the decontamination unit and would be required to go forward to treat wounded soldiers caught in a chemical attack. 'There's no sense in having a female out here when it's pretty clear she can't accomplish as much as a man can, and can't compete in strength.' Having said this, she admitted, 'If they need me I'll have to go and I want to go. This is the furthest women have been in the combat zone. I want everyone to know the part I played, because when it happens I'll have been right in the middle of it.'

Some support units decided to leave their women behind when they were ordered to the Gulf. The Marine Corps had been slow to deploy them, believing that they would be going to war within a short time of arriving. But the decision to post them to the front caused misgivings among some male Marines who complained that despite the women's claims to be the equal of their colleagues, they were given special treatment. They also added with ponderous chivalry that if fighting broke out, male Marines would be distracted by concern for their female comrades. Some small concessions had been made to gender. The women at the base had their own latrines and hooches, and their own hours at the showers. At the mess hall and in their work places they were treated with fraternal courtliness.

Corporal Perez agreed that their presence could cause ripples in the macho surface of Marine front-line life. 'It's a big adjustment for the guys,' she said. 'There's a lot of things they have to hold back on, like swearing. And sex. When men are living in the desert their loins start tingling,' she declared. 'They see a female and their heads aren't clear.

They want to go into combat with a clear head. Having women around can be a pain in the butt.'

Most of the Marines seemed to be in their early to mid-twenties with the interests of their age. They read Stephen King and played pocket video-games, chomped potato chips and Oreos chocolate biscuits irrigated by Coke – the 'hoagy bait' they bought in mounds from the PX store on the base. Despite this uniform modernity they still showed a considerable interest in, and knowledge of, the Corps legends. We shared our tent with Corporal Beard. He had eschewed a mere 'zero to three' and had all his hair shaved off, a look he claimed was 'great with babes'.

Corporal Beard entertained his comrades with pictures of his girlfriends in various states of undress and homespun observations about our predicament. 'I can't believe it,' he cried one day as we were both looking out over the eternal sands. 'The biggest fucking desert in the world and you can't get a beer.' In the States, he declared, 'a swimming pool would have appeared by now, full of babes and Budweiser.' Each evening Corporal Beard would lie down on his cot and resume his study of the biography of Lewis 'Chesty' Puller. Puller was the paradigm of Marine gutsiness, who had stormed through innumerable campaigns, picking up medals and shrapnel fragments, loved by his men and feared by politicians.

As Beard lay there reading, the other Marines would tease him. 'How many guys has Chesty killed now?' they would ask.

Beard would wave his hand testily, 'Shut up. Don't mock the guy.'

Indeed there were few signs that levity concerning the military would be tolerated. One day we were supposed to visit the legal office where soldiers could make their wills. This, someone suggested, had the makings of a brilliant Country and Western song: a maudlin number recounted over a gloomy steel guitar backing track in the gruesome tradition of Wink Martindale's 'Deck of Cards'.

The song's setting would describe the narrator passing by the legal office and noticing over the shoulder of the clerk the last testament of a young warrior flickering on the VDU. As the idea gained ground among the colleagues, lyrics began to emerge. A la Wink Martindale, the song would start off with something like, 'I was walking past the legal office the other day when a strange and touching sight came to my eyes, There on the computer screen was the will of a soldier boy, about to go forth into battle.' Struggling to suppress the emotion in his voice the narrator would then list the details. 'To my Dad I leave the hunting rifle he gave me as a twelve-year-old boy, to my best friend Billy Bob I give the keys of the old Chevvy in which we shared so many good times, to my sweetheart Jolene I bequeath the deeds of the house I bought for her, but which we will never share. . . .'

But what should happen next? Con Coughlin suggested how the story line should develop: the hero goes into action and is reported missing, presumed dead. In fact he is badly wounded, legless as a result of a cluster bomb dropped by his own side. Somehow he struggles home and turns up at the house expecting an ecstatic welcome. His ma breaks the bad news: Billy Bob, who stayed at home during the war, has run off with Jolene. In fact they are now ensconced in the intended matrimonial home. The hero grabs the hunting rifle given to him as a twelve-year-old boy, somehow pilots the old Chevvy down to the house which he bought but would never share, and blows away the faithless couple.

When we recounted the idea for the song we were met with blank stares and cold silences. It was hardly surprising, as things turned out. The prospect of being zapped by your own side was no joke, indeed all too likely. The Pentagon admitted five months after the war was over that almost a quarter of the 148 US servicemen who died in the Gulf War were killed by their own side.

At the time the joke was falling flat, the idea that a mere 148 American lives would be expended in the battles that lay ahead would have seemed absurdly optimistic. The Marines prepared and trained for the worst. At the two field hospitals being built at our base, the medics were expecting a wave of psychological casualties.

One day I was given a tour by a US Navy Lieutenant, a clinical psychologist attached to the Marines. What in the First World War was called 'shell shock', and in the Second 'battle fatigue', had now been designated 'combat stress reaction'. The lieutenant had the cheerfully pessimistic outlook characteristic of many of his calling. He predicted that the hard living conditions, the threat of chemical warfare and the devastating nature of modern warfare would increase dramatically the psychological strain on the troops taking part. 'Potentially we will be inundated with stress victims,' he declared.

Indeed, stress victims were expected to make up the second or third largest number of casualties. The lieutenant enthusiastically detailed the stages of decline: in its mildest form the condition meant that the sufferer would experience difficulty in firing his weapon, could only act under direction and would largely stop functioning in a militarily useful way. At the extreme level he would become a positive liability, losing bowel control and rolling up into the foetal position. The treatment was to take sufferers out of the fighting for seventy-two hours of sleep, food and rest. Then they would be shunted back to the front. The lieutenant emphasised that the victims would be returned to their units as quickly as possible.

Hearing the lieutenant, I was reminded of a British Navy psychologist I'd met on the *Canberra*, the troopship that carried the Royal Marines and the Paras to the Falklands. He, too, was full of dire predictions about the psychological devastation that lay ahead. And he, too, emphasised the importance of the victims being left in no doubt they were heading straight back to the fighting – by ensuring that their rifles never left their sides. His predictions had turned out to be inaccurate. I suspected that in this conflict the conventional psycho-wisdom would be proved wrong again.

At one level, the vivid descriptions of the potential horrors lying ahead served a useful purpose. The Marines' conception of the violence of warfare was partly, maybe largely, derived from television and films. The instructors took great pains to disabuse their charges of any notion that the conflict was going to be a real-life staging of an Arnold Schwarzenegger movie. The first obstacle in the path of the allied army was the swathe of defences stretching around Kuwait City. These had by now been fixed firmly in the imaginations of soldiers and journalists alike, thanks to the military briefers. Their descriptions suggested a fabled construction of antiquity. One pictured elaborate, cliff-like sand walls, lakes of black oil awaiting ignition, huge tracts of sand littered with mines and tank-traps, barbed wire stretching as far as the eye could see.

The crossing was clearly going to be hell, an impression reinforced by the instructors. One bitterly cold morning I went out to see a sergeant take a group of combat engineers through a mine-clearing drill. 'The reason for this is so when your buddy disappears in a big pink mist and body parts are flying, you'll know what to do,' he told them in a hectoring Boot Camp manner.

He stared belligerently at a Marine who had augmented his issue weapons with a dagger. 'All you Rambos with knives dangling from your gear. If you're with me and one of those things falls off and hits a mine, I'm going to crawl out on my bloody stumps and choke you out.'

A few days later, on 30 January, the Marines got their first real taste of combat. We were standing in the chow-line on a sunny early morning when the rumour went round that the Iraqis had launched an audacious offensive the night before. It had failed and a group of Iraqi tanks was now surrounded, somewhere near the camp motor pool. Our public-affairs minder dismissed the chow-line version as fantasy. We insisted that he check it out. As we were frequently to discover, the chow-line had been first with the news, or at least an approximation of it. We learned from the Intelligence officer at the General's HQ that the Iraqis had indeed launched a series of surprise attacks across the Saudi border. The manoeuvre had been on three main axes. In one action, Marine Light Armoured Vehicles – supported by helicopters and jets – had successfully destroyed an Iraqi column moving south in the Qua'ara area, just inside the Saudi border. In another engagement a Saudi battalion had beaten off a thrust by a platoon of Iraqi tanks. But on the coast the Iraqis had been more successful. Under cover of darkness a smallish force had taken Khafji, whose defence had been left for obvious political reasons to the Saudis. It seemed strange to think of the town in Iraqi hands. It was a spread-out, unlovely place, largely evacuated by the time of the incursion but it had a reasonable hotel, the Khafji Beach, where we had stopped several times for lunch after a morning at the border.

By the time we arrived at the outskirts of the town, confusion reigned. We were stopped a few kilometres from the entrance by a contingent of Marines who said Khafji was now surrounded by coalition forces, including Saudi National Guardsmen and Qataris, and everything was quiet. There were mixed reports about whether the Iraqis were still there or had beaten a retreat before dawn. We stood at the side of the road, a blustery wind whipping in from the sea. At one point a column of Humvees with TOW missiles, heavy machine guns and grenade launchers mounted on top, set off to investigate a report that unidentified vehicles were approaching. They never found them. By now artillery had been brought up. The air wobbled as the batteries of 155mm howitzers opened up. Occasionally a smudge of black smoke, emerging over the roofs of the town, would announce where a round had landed. From the Iraqis there was no response.

Then at eleven forty-five an excited report on the radio

net passed on the startling information that the Saudis had spotted a force of up to eighty Iraqi vehicles and perhaps 4,000 troops advancing on the Khafji area from the north. 'Apparently they want to surrender,' said the major in charge. 'They have their turrets reversed and they are not indicating any hostile intent.' As the Saudi National Guard prepared to go forward to accept the surrender, the major was concerned that the Saudis might be panicked into opening fire. 'We've got to play this close to our vest,' he said. 'We don't want to blow it.'

But barely ten minutes later, another very different report came over the radio. The major listened intently. 'They have engaged the Saudi forces,' he said. 'And we're going to kill them.'

In fact this turned out to be an over-optimistic forecast from the allied point of view. When we left in the late afternoon, information was sketchy but it seemed that the battle was more or less over. When we awoke the following day, it transpired that the Iraqis had yet to be dislodged from the town. It was not until the afternoon that the Saudis, who had been heavily supported throughout by the Americans and Qataris, finally retook the place after thirty-six hours of occupation. The Americans put the best face on it they could. It was evidence of Saddam's military stupidity, they said. The fact that Khafji had been barely defended was brushed aside. It was conventional doctrine that you didn't defend a border town in strength when an occupying army was just over the border, everyone knew that. At best Saddam had achieved a *coup de théâtre*. This, indeed, is what it looked like – the sort of cosmetic triumph that could be played up in the state media, a welcome morale booster as the bombs were raining on Baghdad and Basra. The fact that several hundred of his men were sacrificed in the gesture would of course have meant nothing to Saddam.

Shortly before Khafji finally fell we went to see the commander of the US Marines in the Gulf, General Walt

Boomer. The General fitted, to an extraordinary degree, the popular ideal of the soldier. He was tall, and moved with forceful, sweeping grace. There was a touch of Jack Pallance about the lean face and the flat stomach on the fifty-two-year-old body. His speech, though, was precise and un-theatrical and unsurprising. The incursion had had 'zero' effect, necessitating only a few minor adjustments to his line. He believed it was 'a time for patience. In my view the air campaign is working. I never believed it would be as quick as some thought it would be . . . we're not in a hurry.'

General Boomer – the name sounded like a fire-eating dragoon in a Restoration comedy – was a Vietnam veteran with two tours behind him as a field commander and as a military adviser to the South Vietnamese forces. He was happy with the way the military had been allowed to get on with its task. There was none of the 'micro-management' that accepted military wisdom now blames for crippling the American effort in Indo-China. 'I don't sense there's any holding back on our part,' he said. 'Except what you would expect us to do anyway and that is to protect innocent civilians to the extent that you possibly can . . . that's the only thing I see as a restriction.' Before we left he warned that the pounding that they had been receiving in the air-war had so far been relatively kind to the Iraqi soldiers sitting over the border in their trenches. 'The guys in front can expect the worst and the worst is yet to come.' On the other hand, despite the morale problems evident from the slow trickle of deserters crossing the line, 'we don't underestimate the guy either. I think he'll fight.'

It seemed hard to imagine what could be done to the Iraqis that was not already happening to them. Each night we heard the virtually continuous drone of the bombers high overhead. The soldiers watched with awe the great flashes of light on the horizon and felt pity for those underneath. We knew how the latter must be reacting from the behaviour of the Iraqi deserters and prisoners. During air-raids, their captors reported, they would roll up in the foetal position.

The Marines showed little animosity towards their enemy. In fact 'enemy' was a word you rarely heard except on the lips of the rear-echelon administrators sitting comfortably in Dhahran. The ordinary soldiers seemed to regard the opposition as simple soldiers, just doing their job, victims in their way of Saddam Hussein. Often the deeds of the Iraqis were ascribed exclusively to their leader, as in 'Saddam invaded Kuwait' or 'Saddam attacked Khafji'. In a curious way the allied soldiers felt closer to their opponents than they did to their Saudi hosts. No one seemed to buy the official line that the National Guard had played a sterling part in the retaking of Khafji. The Marines were inclined to regard them rather as their grandfathers had regarded the Italians in the Second World War, ready to 'haul ass' as soon as the going got tough.

At the base the feeling of movement was in the air. There were rumours that the entire camp, so laboriously assembled, was about to up sticks and move to a different location. As fact superseded rumour, the prospect of the ground war loomed more threateningly. Down at the PX store the lines lengthened as the troops stocked up with comforting 'hoagy bait'. The custom at the tented church picked up, too. One Sunday I went to the Catholic Mass. Afterwards I stood chatting with three men from the grave detachment, charged with the task of gathering up and identifying remains, a particularly horrible job in modern warfare. 'In normal circumstances I don't go to Mass,' said a young sergeant from Georgia. 'I don't need the extra lift. Here I do.'

As we trudged back across the sand my companion, Mike Sullivan the American reporter who had served in the Marines, remembered a maxim from his Vietnam days. 'There are no atheists in a foxhole.'

106

CHAPTER SEVEN

Although it was only I and Charles Richards of the *Independent* who had been selected for membership of the pool, as the ground war grew closer, pressure mounted among the horde of new arrivals back in Dhahran to rotate the pool and bring the Brits back. This struck Charles and myself as unfair. What was the point of hanging around in the desert, rising at dawn, turning in at dusk in a tent full of burping, snoring men for a freezing night on a hard cot, cut off from communication with the outside world, if at the last minute a TV crew from Tokyo came in to cover the war? I protested vigorously. But something seemed to have happened back in Dhahran. The public-relations colonel who had previously been charm itself was distant and finally rude when I presented my case in person. I was not to return to the desert. Someone else – a 'Brit' as it turned out – was going to take my place.

I felt aggrieved for a while, then relieved. The pool had advantages: notably that it gave you a guaranteed seat at the hostilities when they began, which was the point of all the waiting of the preceding seven months. You had constant access to the officers and men. But set against this were the great difficulty in communications and the restrictions of censorship. The Americans had deliberately prevented journalists from making their own arrangements for transmitting their copy, film or video tape. The network reporters were denied their satellite dishes, the newspaper correspondents, their satellite phones. Everything had to be handed to a military courier, none of whom seemed overburdened with a sense of urgency, to drive back to base four hours away. There the copy might sit disregarded until one of the censors returned from the coffee shop. In a lightning war these delays could render one's efforts useless.

Control of communications of course strengthened the military's grip on information. The question of censorship became something of an obsession both for the military and for the media members themselves. So seriously did the military regard the potential of the media, particularly television, to do good or harm, and so seriously did the media take itself, that questions about the way the war was being covered attained almost as much importance as discussion of the way the war was being fought.

The censorship debate was an old one. I had been through it during and after the Falklands War. Now it was resumed with even greater energy, carried aloft by the swelling clouds of media self-importance that had blown up in the intervening nine years. The proposition was made in some quarters that the pool system was almost entirely iniquitous, that its members were fed only what the military wished to give them, that reporters ceased to apply their critical faculties and ended up as mere propagandists for the organisation to which they were attached.

I felt it was important that someone was on the pool, as a duty to history. Restrictions or censorship might prevent a reporter filing a story hostile to the interests of the military on the day of the event. But his or her presence virtually ensured that it would get out afterwards. It seemed naïve to expect the military to share the media's estimate of the boundaries of their rights. The notion of having its affairs aired in public – unless specifically guaranteed to bring glory to individual or unit – ran completely against military thinking. Though they might express it more diplomatically, most soldiers shared the view of an old gunnery sergeant made during a discussion of a proposal by one of the anti-censorship tribunes that journalists should be allowed to roam the front line unfettered: 'If they came anywhere near me I would shoot the bastards.'

Whatever its advantages, to most newspaper reporters the pool just didn't feel right. It was more the social than the professional restrictions that got one down. A few days in a Marine camp is a forceful reminder of why one never considered a military career. The regimentation of every aspect of life, the suspicion of initiative, the enforced camaraderie: all quickly put paid to any romanticism concerning the nature of martial life.

The television people were happy. The essential meaningless of most of what they were filming did not bother them. The fact that the tank blasting away in front of them was on a training exercise and not engaging the enemy was neither here nor there. It was a good picture, that would look great on the evening news.

Most of the military were TV people, even the oldest belonged to a generation who grew up bathed in the distorting light of the cathode-ray tube. Despite the Vietnam experience they were well disposed towards the correspondents and crews, happy to help out in the relentless hunt for pictures, secretly hopeful of the fame the association might bring. No group of people with the exception of film stars and pop singers craves fame more than the military.

The newspaper correspondents were different. There were a number who regarded themselves as unpaid propagandists for the army or the Marine Corps, and who were morbidly afraid of breaching regulations or giving offence. But most found that aspect irksome, an unwelcome plunge back into the bondage of rules and regulations from which the practice of journalism provides an escape.

For the newspaper correspondents on our pool, the wall of restrictions soon wore away our surface aquiescence to reveal the thick seam of bolshiness that runs through most print hacks. There are two phrases that superiors hate to hear. One is 'Why?' The other is 'Why not?' During my time with the Marines there were regular shouting matches between the print journalists and our minder – a decent, intelligent, well-meaning man who strove hard to see our point of view when we questioned the value of the myriad restrictions.

On the day after the Khafji incursion, we pressed to return to the battle zone only to be told it was the province of another pool team and therefore out of bounds. After another shouting match, our minder relented and agreed that we could go. As we drove up the coast road we saw fleets of non-pool journalists heading in the same direction. 'Don't worry, they'll be turned back,' he promised.

But when we arrived at the checkpoint outside the town, a large media gathering was already in place. Our lieutenant was quivering with rage. He jumped out of the Land Cruiser, pulled out a notebook and started taking people's names, threatening them with expulsion from Saudi Arabia if they didn't clear off. As they climbed into their cars and drove away they had the look of a rebel band, joyfully retiring to the hills while the flat-footed conscripts gazed glumly at their retreating backs. It was going too far to say that Dhahran, base of the non-pool journalists, offered any of the romance of a rebel headquarters – no campfires, no girl guerrillas strumming guitars as the whisky went round. In fact Dhahran was the dullest place I had ever been to in the world. Nonetheless it felt more like home than the pool. I was being booted out of the government barracks anyway. There was no choice but to return to the sierras.

By the time I got back I found that the rebel camp had moved. The vast network entourages had stayed in Dhahran, as well as a number of newspaper and radio reporters charged with presenting the overall picture. But the more adventurous spirits had shifted northwards, to the border town of Hafr al Battin. Hafr was ideally placed as a base for

110

the 'unilaterals' as the military authorities had designated non-pool journalists who nonetheless tried to cover events in the desert. It lay at the western end of the front line, astride a main road used by the allies as one of the main supply routes. It had a frontier feel. The pavements were elevated, like in a Western. It had a sense of bustle completely lacking in most Saudi towns, largely as a consequence of the large Asian population who ran the shops and garages.

In the middle of the main street was the Fao Hotel, which had been adopted as the Unilaterals' headquarters. When I arrived it seemed that it was under military, rather than journalistic, occupation. Walking into the lobby I saw a number of purposeful, noisy men dressed in a variety of uniforms. Looking more closely, I recognised some familiar faces. There was Colin Smith of the *Observer*, dressed in Guernsey, well-pressed fatigues and desert boots – a look redolent of the gymkhana club or a colonial officers' mess. With him was Derek Hudson, the Sygma photographer, whose dashing green *shamal*, teamed with his camouflage uniform, hinted at Special Forces affiliations. David Williams of the *Daily Mail* was rigged out in full British desert gear. Jon Swain from the *Sunday Times* was wearing an anti-chemical suit, with green-netting cravat accessory. Others had been less successful in counterfeiting the military look. Several of the company were wearing boiler suits, overalls, anything with a patch pocket or an epaulette, in an effort at disguise which suggested a gas station forecourt rather than the battlefield.

Journalists are traditionally against the idea of dressing up as soldiers. In the Falklands we had argued briefly for wearing fluorescent anoraks so that the Argentinians would know we were non-combatants. Then it was pointed out that this would merely ensure that we were the first to be shot by the snipers. In this instance, though, the uniforms were close to a necessity. Hafr al Battin was out of bounds. The Saudi authorities had repeatedly warned that anyone found there faced expulsion from the country or at least 'having their credentials removed' – a phrase that always carried an unpleasant implication of amputation, or worse.

The roads around the town were crawling with military policemen (MPs) who were only too happy to arrest any journalists disobeying the instruction. It had already happened several times. A luckless photographer had been arrested by an MP from Alabama. The photographer explained that he was a fellow-American simply doing his job, but the MP had his doubts. Suspecting him of espionage, he began questioning him about obscure Southern sporting events. Who was the winner of the recent football game between the Tampa Bay Falcons and the Miami Dophins? When the photographer failed to answer correctly, he was thrown into a cell and held overnight.

Wearing a uniform did not necessarily protect one from being arrested. Needless to say it had been specifically prohibited by the Saudi authorities, so in one way it actually deepened the heinousness of the offence of being out of bounds. But military kit helped us to blend in with the surroundings. Every foreigner was wearing it. To the average Saudi soldier manning a roadblock, one white man in camouflage was much the same as another and, thanks to the alcohol-free regime imposed by Saudi laws, and the long hours on the tennis courts of the Dhahran Meridien waiting for something to happen, most journalists looked in physically similar shape to their military contemporaries. At the same time if you were wearing American kit in a British area you were likely to escape challenge and vice versa. I kept my American uniform from my pool duty, as well as a Department of Defense identity card that was virtually identical to the standard military issue. In order to gain a bit of flexibility I also bought khaki trousers and a military-looking khaki shirt. With some webbing and the Ray Bans, I felt I could plausibly pass myself off as a French officer serving in some obscure capacity.

Along with the correct attire it was vital to have the right vehicle. The preferred motor was a four-wheel-drive Toyota Land Cruiser, though Smith and Hudson – carrying verisimilitude to fanatical lengths – had bought a British army-style khaki-coloured Land Rover which they festooned with camouflage netting.

Hundreds of Toyotas had been requisitioned by the allies to augment their transport. All we had to do to make our vehicles look the same was to copy the inverted v-shape markings the soldiers had taped on the sides and bonnets of the Land Cruisers, and find some fluorescent material to tie to the roof. The marker-strip seemed a good idea. It was meant to tell the pilots overhead that you were on their side. Initially, fluorescent material was in short supply. The nearest thing I could find to it in the Shula Centre in Dhahran was an orange day-glo inflatable Yogi Bear and a yellow BooBoo. I bought two Yogis and one BooBoo and distributed them among colleagues. The next day we set off to Hafr with them flapping from the roofs. As the four-hour journey progressed, the knots became looser and looser. Eventually they were mercifully torn from the vehicles and swept off into the desert.

Seasoned unilaterals, who had had a week or two in the field, had adapted enthusiastically to the imposture. Two reporters had been stopped by a couple of Desert Rats who apologetically asked directions to their position. The journalists, got up in a meticulous travesty of British uniform, right down to phoney cap badges, barked instructions in strangled Sandhurst accents and sent them on their way.

Roaming around the border road, ducking and diving, was an unsatisfactory way of doing things, but at least the unilaterals were nibbling at the edges of the story. A little to the east of Hafr was the British Seventh Armoured Brigade Headquarters, where several of our pool colleagues were based. They were having a boring time. Confined to the

113

camp, they were reduced to a steady stream of 'the waiting is almost over' despatches.

One day Richard Dowden of the *Independent* scored a major scoop when a group of Iraqi deserters surrendered to him. By this time a steady number of Iraqis were giving themselves up every day. There came a morning when we drove up to al Ruqi, the border post on the Kuwaiti frontier due north of Hafr. Ruqi was in the Egyptian sector of the line, and the Egyptians, friendliest of people, were always prepared to overlook the rules and give journalists a welcome. We drove into the camp, sat down with a medical lieutenant and a captain, drank tea and exchanged cigarettes. It took a while for us to notice the dirty, exhausted group of men sitting in a corner of the camp. We walked over. They were stretched out on blankets in the sun, like tired old dogs. The pile of boots lying by the side of them provided eloquent evidence of the state of the army they had left behind. They were scuffed and broken. Some of them had no heels. Among them was a dilapidated pair of Chelsea boots, the sort of thing the young men of Baghdad wear on summer evenings sauntering down Rashid Street. Whoever owned them was a long way from Rashid Street now.

There were twelve of them, ranging from a man in his mid-forties to a boy in his teens, all privates with the Iraqi 27th Division: a pretty representative cross-section, as it turned out, of the men opposing the allied armies in the trenches opposite. The night before, with the allied air force droning on endless sorties overhead, they had slipped away from their posts and crawled through minefields on their bellies to avoid being spotted by their own, or the allied, sentries. The five-kilometre journey to the Egyptian positions had taken them four hours. While some dozed on the blankets, the others were chatting and laughing with the guards.

'We came because we didn't want to die,' said Ali, a

114

twenty-two-year-old with four days' stubble on his cheeks and a crumpled Soviet-issue cap on his head. 'Every day there is bombing and artillery. A few of us have died but we are well dug in. The planes have been destroying our guns, but we are well dug in.' The deserters' stories seemed to match up with what allied Intelligence was saying. Ali reported that they ate only once a day, a few spoonfuls of bread and rice. 'It's not enough for soldiers.' Six of the twelve had fought in the eight-year war with Iran and were still in uniform when they were thrown into this conflict.

'When we fought Iran we had breakfast, dinner and water but here we have nothing,' said one. 'There it was an army against an army. Here all we see are bombs.'

From my memory of the Iraqi front-line in the Basra sector during the war, conditions had not been too bad. The bunkers had grown quite homely over the years. The inhabitants had built proper beds, installed televisions and put carpets on the floor. The troops did short tours and were rotated regularly. They were fighting on home territory and, as I knew from that distant New Year's Eve in the Basra nightclub, were free to enjoy themselves with a spot of R and R.

According to Ali, all the soldiers wanted to desert but were afraid to because of the minefields they had laid in front of their positions. In the event this assessment was entirely correct. 'We don't believe in the war,' he declared with loud sincerity. 'We don't want to fight our brother Muslims. Kuwaitis are our brothers, but Kuwait is Kuwait and Iraq is Iraq.'

This seemed to be an accurate summing up of how most of the Arab troops felt. The notion of Arab brotherhood remained strong despite the situation but so, too, did belief in the inviolability of the independence of nations. Like their Western comrades, they tended to blame Saddam for all Iraqi wrongdoings. 'I don't want to see Iraq destroyed,' said Ahmad, the Egyptian army doctor. 'I want to liberate

115

Kuwait. I only want to fight Iraq until Kuwait is liberated.'

His boss Major Magdi said, 'I want no war at all. We want peace.'

The Arab armies were strung out in a line on both sides of the border road stretching west from al Ruqi. After the Egyptians came the Syrians. They were much less friendly, watching us suspiciously from their tanks and armoured personnel vehicles with Hafez al Assad's 'Big Brother' features stencilled on the side, as we cruised up and down the road. Next were the Shahid (Martyr) Brigade of the Kuwaiti army. Their camp was a picture of timeless military squalor. There were live lambs tethered to the tent pegs and dead ones turning on spits over charcoal fires. The soldiers wandered around in brown sheepskin-lined cloaks that reached down to their ankles. Mounds of discarded condensed-milk and soft-drink tins littered the sand. Inside the tents the soldiers lay around on carpets, smoking *nargilehs* and listening to tunes played on *rababas* – miniature cellos – made out of old oil cans.

For symbolic purposes it was planned that the Kuwaitis were to be the first into Kuwait City. It was clear after five minutes in the camp that they could not be relied on to do any serious fighting. For a few brief hours it seemed that fighting by the ground troops might not in fact be required. On 16 February an announcement from Baghdad suggested that Saddam was ready to withdraw from Kuwait. CNN showed ecstatic Baghdadis firing their rifles in the air in relief. Then within an hour the apparent offer was qualified. A stream of conditions was attached.

The manoeuvre had failed to slow down allied operations by a minute. While inside the Dharan JIB, the pundits on the eternally playing televisions debated the significance of the development, outside the jets were continuing to roar off the runway from the airbase next door.

Many of us had decided to leave Hafr for the weekend because of a rumour that the Saudi authorities were planning to send a raiding party to round up the unilaterals. They had already published a list detailing forbidden practices, such as wearing uniforms, leaving the Dhahran area without permission: we were breaking all of them. The prospect of a posse from the JIB, bursting into the Fao in their *thobes* and *qutras*, was rather exciting. The Fao, with its rickety wooden staircase and first floor balconies overlooking the street, was the perfect setting for a Western showdown. There were many cinematic possibilities, a last stand perhaps with the desperate unilaterals hurling their tormentors through the matchwood banisters or, alternatively, prudent flight, with the hacks dropping lightly from the upper storeys into the street, then mounting their trusty Toyotas and roaring off. In fact the JIB men never came. On reflection it seemed highly unlikely that a Saudi official was going to do anything as fatiguing as expelling a bunch of journalists from a hotel. Particularly not on a Friday. On Sunday we went back.

The roads up to and along the border were choked with vehicles ferrying petrol, water, ammunition and supplies to the troops in the front line. It seemed incredible that they should require any more. Yet the convoys rolled night and day. All along the routes lay the wrecks of cars and lorries, crumpled like discarded Coke cans.

Everyone was moving. The allied line was shifting to the West. In the desert huge curtains of tawny dust hung in the air, churned up by mass migrations of armour. Overnight, large bases were dismantled, packed away and reassembled scores of kilometres to the West, leaving behind only sand berms and bunkers.

On Tuesday 19 February I drove with Chris Harris, *The Times* photographer, along the highway from Hafr al Battin to the town of Rafah, close to the Saudi frontier with Iraq at the far end of the 600-kilometre-long front line. On the other side of the road for virtually all the way, there was an unbroken succession of military bases. There were logistics bases, brimming with material; communications centres

117

bristling with antennae and dishes; parks crammed with tanks and light armour. Further back in the desert the tanks lurking under their camouflage netting could just be made out. At one point a section of the road had been sealed off to serve as a runway for transport planes. As we drove past, a couple of Hercules C130s were on the tarmac preparing to take off, while another one was landing and parking its fat belly on the ground with surprising grace. A little further away six giant Chinook helicopters moved in formation across the desert fifteen metres above the ground, smoothly rising and falling like horses in a fairground carousel.

On some stretches of the road, the traffic was bumper to giant bumper. Inside the cabs the drivers leaned forward over their wheels, blank-faced, grim-looking, with piratical bandannas knotted around their heads. The American trucks had nicknames . . . 'New York Puta' . . . 'The Fridge'. . . . The Filipino trucks had cracker-barrel messages of hope and happiness . . . 'East West Home's Best' . . . 'In God We Trust'.

The town itself was full of allied troops. One shopkeeper had put up a sign saying, 'From here you can telephone to France.' Outside, the lean young men of the French contingent based nearby were lining up to pass on some last endearments to the wife or girlfriend and to tell their mothers and fathers not to worry. Down the street on the corner of the main drag, the Americans were doing the same. In the mini-markets, soldiers were emptying the shelves of chocolates, biscuits and cigarettes. Everyone looked sombre and preoccupied. I started chatting with a pair of Frenchmen. They seemed distracted when I asked them about war preparations but perked up when I mentioned I was thinking of buying a house in the Tarn. One of the two was from Albi. He talked enthusiastically about property prices for a while, no doubt glad to be reminded of the more permanent reality over the horizon. But the happiest people in Rafah were the children. The arrival of

the soldiers had brought about an unimaginable transforma-
tion of their dreary town whose backstreets were parched
and windswept, the houses hidden by high walls. By Saudi
standards they were slums. The wild little kids ran about in
high spirits, kicking footballs around, shouting 'Hallo' and
giving the thumbs-up sign to every allied vehicle rolling past.

Within the next few days the soldiers would go and Rafah
would return to its tedious normality, the tanks and Humvees, the large, pale strangers would become a memory,
albeit one the children would probably never lose.

On the way back we kept coming across concentrations of
troops and materiel we had not noticed on our approach
journey. Once, we crested a hill and looked down – like
James Bond peering into the villain's secret volcano-crater
base – into a *wadi*, swirling with dust, where lorries raced to
and fro in little bursts of inexplicable activity. Occasionally
we could hear in the distance the flat, door-slamming noise
of an outgoing shell. It was nothing compared with the bombardment that we expected in the near future. The acquaint-
ances we had made among the British soldiers who came to
Hafr al Battin to shop for luxuries, and who dropped by the
Fao Hotel to call home, were forecasting a massive artillery
bombardment that would rain shells on the Iraqi positions
along the length of the line before the operation began.

A more immediate sign of the impending attack could be
seen up on the border. Two days after going to Rafah we
went up to Ruqi. As we arrived, a bulldozer was making its
way up to the berm, the great double wall of sand five metres
high and ten metres wide, that runs along the Saudi frontier.
Operations were being supervised by a Saudi building con-
tractor we knew from the Fao. He liked to drop by at night,
dressed in an approximation of martial gear which he felt
suitable for the times. The most striking feature was a pair
of welding goggles, slung Rommel-fashion around his neck.
He stood up in his truck, waving on the bulldozer as it reared

and dipped its way through the sand. With a last noisy heave it broke through and there lay the Kuwaiti plain, just as sandy, boring and devoid of cover as the terrain from which we were watching.

Behind us the Egyptian tanks revved and belched smoke and clanked forward to take up positions around the breach. Overhead the usual air activity was going on, generating the usual feeling of unreality. The B52s were high but distinctly visible, their huge swept-back wings swimming slowly through the sky like malevolent fish glimpsed distantly through a glass-bottomed boat. Then, there was the distant roll of high-explosives. Then, the smoke – white and pretty at first – quickly turning black and sinister. From the other side there was nothing, not even a single, symbolic artillery-round fired in our direction in protest. It was hard now to believe that the Iraqis were keeping their powder dry, hard to go along with General Boomer's assessment that 'the guy is going to fight'. The only contact the Egyptians had with their opponents was through the deserters, straggling in over the sands.

The Egyptians had lost some of their nonchalance. The colonel in charge of the operation, Mamdoeh al Koney, was unhappy about what lay ahead. 'If they surrender, we will be pleased,' he said. 'If they do otherwise, they will be shot down. It is one life for another.' The prospect of killing Arabs filled him with gloom. 'I can't imagine why this man has created this mess,' he said. 'He is a man of no principle. We are one people with a shared culture, ideals and language. Iraq is a strong country, we need Iraq.' He paused. 'But if you have an illness in one part of you, it affects the whole body. We don't want to kill them but. . . .' Like all the Egyptians he was filled with contempt for Saddam's pretensions to be another Nasser. 'How can he kill his people like this?' he said. 'Nasser would never have done this. He stopped the six-day war because people were dying.'

By this time the Iraqis were saying in Baghdad that the ground war had already started. If it hadn't, it was clearly

120

about to. The following day was a Saturday. David Williams'
army friends came by the hotel to make their final calls
home. While there, they told us the marking we should put
on our vehicles, '1/1/HQ', to avoid challenge and advised us
to fix red lights in the rear windows. Later in the morning
we drove up to see the Egyptians at Rugi to try and persuade
them to take us along with them when they attacked. We
were ushered in to see a colonel. He spoke no English but
one of his staff who spoke French acted as a translator. The
colonel was friendly but suspicious. He asked us what we
knew about the battle plan. I began repeating what we had
picked up. He asked me to demonstrate the moves on the
map on the wall. I found myself confidently detailing thrusts,
feints, helicopter-borne assaults, in front of a rapt audience.
The colonel was impressed. His suspicions, he said, were
justified. The claim to be journalists was a pretence, we were
clearly army officers. Shaking his head in amusement at the
mysterious ways of the British, he ushered us out. If we
wanted to travel with the Egyptians we would have to go
and see his general.

The rest of the day was spent in a state of anxiety as we
rehearsed over and over again the likely scenarios of how
events would unfold and how we would cover them. Our only
option seemed to be to attach ourselves to some element of
the attacking forces and hope that in the confusion no one had
the time to arrest us. In this respect the Egyptians seemed to
offer the best prospect. The thought of the bureaucracy
involved in obtaining some sort of accreditation from the general filled us with gloom. It was better to trust to fate and hope
it would all be all right on the day.

The hotel was now full of journalists. Most of them were
British or French. Americans for some reason did not loom
large in the ranks of the unilaterals. The few that were
around had a dazed, preoccupied look. Among them was a
reporter from an obscure Washington business magazine and
his photographer, a camp figure wearing a Sheikh of Araby

silk headscarf, who lectured his hard-bitten French and British colleagues on where they were going wrong in their coverage. Nationalities tended to stick together: the French at one table, the British at another, though we regarded each other as natural allies against the Americans. The restaurant was packed with reporters and camera men, eating pizza and drinking alcohol-free beer. There was an atmosphere of excitement and anticipation. We felt nervous at being out of touch. The war could start and we would know nothing about it.

A group of us decided to drive back to Ruqi to see if anything was going on. We parked in a derelict petrol station near the border-post. It was a cold night. A rusty sign squeaked in the wind. The cry was taken up by three wild cats lurking by the pumps. On the radio the BBC newsreader was giving the latest details of the last-minute Soviet diplomatic initiative to avert the war. All the time in the background we could hear the thump of outgoing artillery, interspersed with the *whoosh*, like a giant broom being pushed across a yard, of the multiple-rocket launchers.

There was something odd about the sky. The western side of the horizon was clear, the stars twinkling with that stunning Arabian lustre. But on the eastern side there were no stars to be seen. The air seemed to be filled with a dark haze that spread even as we watched it. The smoke was coming from the direction of the al Burqan oilfield in Kuwait. Saddam had done what he'd promised he would do. We drove back through deepening darkness.

CHAPTER EIGHT

At four o'clock that morning, 24 February, the phone rang in my bedroom. An American journalist asked me If I could tell him what was going on. The ground war had started. I stumbled downstairs. The others were beginning to assemble. We ordered some coffee and resumed the eternal tactical discussion. Chris Harris and I finally decided to head north to Ruqi and along the border road eastwards to see if we could meet up with an American army unit, the Tiger Brigade, which was attached to the Marine Corps on its left flank.

It was drizzling as we drove up to the border and we passed the Egyptian lines, snugly tucked behind the berm. No one seemed to be awake. Fifty kilometres later we came across a concentration of American troops straddling the road. A battery of howitzers was banging away. We went over to the nearest gun. It had been firing all night and the ground around was piled up with plastic shell cases. The black sergeant in charge of the battery was leaning against the howitzer, almost speechless with exhaustion. There had been a few incoming rounds from the Iraqis during the night, he said, but nothing serious. In the circumstances, firing back would require suicidal dedication. Above us A10 Thunderbolt jets were flying low, circling and diving, scanning the ground like birds of prey for any sign of an Iraqi. It was inauspicious weather. During the night there had been a violent thunderstorm and now, rain, wind and scudding cloud had cut visibility down to less than three kilometres.

Eventually the road ran out and we turned onto a desert track. Or tracks. Every few hundred metres the path divided into two equally well-worn forks. Staying as close to the berm as we could, we drove on. Suddenly a column of M1 tanks loomed out of the drizzle, chugging over the damp sand, pennants snapping on their antennae in the stiff wind. Chris leaned a long lens through the window to fire off some shots. Seeing the Land Cruiser, a tank with an ace of spades and a skull painted on the hull swung its gun 180 degrees towards us. For a few seconds we found ourselves looking straight down the barrel. Then apparently satisfied that we were not Iraqi infiltrators it swung away again. The grim-faced commander waved to us and the tank throbbed on its way to the Berm.

A little further on we found Tiger Brigade. They were formed up, waiting for the order to advance. The men were standing around their tanks and APCs, laughing and smoking. Next to them was a Marine TOW platoon. We stopped for a chat. There was a feeling of exhilaration in the air, of relief that at last the battle had begun. 'It's the first step home,' said a sergeant from the Marine Reserves. 'Either toes up or toes down we'll be going home soon.'

All the apprehensions of the days of preparation seemed to have disappeared. 'I've been waiting fourteen years for this,' said a gap-toothed Texan. 'This will weed out the weak of heart and the weak of mind. This is going to end decisively. We're going to chase him down and kill him.' While he was speaking, the background din of engines and distant gunfire was suddenly punctuated by the flat *bob bob bob* of a heavy machine gun.

The Marines looked round startled. A gunner had absent-mindedly squeezed the trigger on the .50-calibre weapon, mercifully missing the vehicles ahead. 'Jesus Christ,' said the gunner sergeant in disgust. 'That is our biggest danger. Friendly fucking fire.'

Eventually, just before noon, a reconnaissance vehicle arrived to tell the platoon that their designated lane through the minefield that lay just beyond the berm was nearly clear. The driver was in high spirits. 'It's only going to need four Marines and box of firelighters to take these guys,' he shouted. The engineers had been firing line charges to detonate the devices buried in the sand, then bulldozing a path through. A report came over the radio that one of the lanes was contaminated after a bulldozer set off a chemical mine. The wind and the rain meant that the threat from chemicals was tiny, but the men were taking no chances. Everyone was wearing their charcoal-impregnated suits and rubber overboots and gloves. Before the column moved off, many of the Marines pulled on their gas masks. At twelve twenty-five the major gave the order to go, and the thirty Humvees, interspersed with M1 tanks, revved their engines and advanced through the Berm and up to the minefield. The path to relative safety was marked out incongruously with bright-blue upturned dustbins. We tagged behind the column and followed it into Kuwait.

The rain had stopped and the sun came out. As they arrived on Kuwaiti soil the TOW gunners, perched on top of their vehicles, punched the air and shouted. There was no sign of the Iraqis. Ahead of us lay what looked like an oil-gathering station and some power lines, part of the Umm Gudair oilfield.

Already the helicopters were flying overhead, bulky loads swaying from the nets slung beneath their bellies. The Marines shouted, 'Stay with us, we're going to be in Kuwait City by this evening.' But we had to go, to get back to Hafr al Battin to file the story and send the pictures. By the time we had crossed back through the Berm and into Saudi Arabia, the armour had already disappeared. A little further back, long columns of trucks and tankers were forming up ready to move into Kuwait. Finding our way back was difficult and we got lost several times before we reached the tarmac road we had turned off that morning. The Arabs had moved up to take the place of the Americans. We passed the Kuwaiti Shahid brigade. Their Chieftain tanks were lined up by the side of the road. The bearded drivers were revving the engines, yelling and waving victory signs at passers-by. These triumphant demonstrations, it turned out, were to constitute Kuwait's most significant military contribution to the allied campaign. Further on, the Egyptians had brought up their artillery and were firing into Kuwait with howitzers and muliple-rocket launchers. Some of the tanks had moved up through the breach in the Berm. The gunners smiled and called out 'Up with Egypt.' The sun was hot now and there was a total absence of any feeling of danger, giving the proceedings an almost festive atmosphere. The Iraqis, lying in the path of the deadly machine threshing towards them in top gear, seemed to have become almost irrelevant.

As we were driving back to Hafr, a number of empty buses passed us coming from the opposite direction. When we arrived at the hotel, David Williams told us that the Iraqis had been surrendering in their thousands.

At the first sight of the allies, they had stumbled out of their positions, some of them crying with relief, all clutching dirty paper handkerchiefs, pieces of white paper and rags tied to sticks in a pathetic gesture of surrender. Extensive preparations had been made to handle prisoners – 500 forty-seat buses were standing by at Hafr – but they were already overwhelmed.

The war was turning into a rout. From the first day of the air-attack, it seemed likely that the Iraqis would put up little resistance. I had seen the Republican Guard in action in the Iran-Iraq war and felt that their stock designation by the allied military and media as élite troops was a great exaggeration. The way things were going it seemed that Kuwait City could fall to the allies within twenty-four hours. Chris and I got up early and returned to Ruqi. We arrived at dawn just in time to see the main force of the Egyptians streaming slowly through the hole that had been bulldozed through the berm a few days before. We joined the column as it trundled along. The Egyptians were tasked with cutting through a sector of the Iraqi fixed positions to the west of the Marines. A few kilometres inside Kuwait the convoy crossed an inviting-looking tarmac road which, if we survived the mines, would have taken us to Kuwait City in ninety minutes. The thought of the mines was very disturbing. I tried as much as possible to keep in the tracks of the vehicles ahead. But once we had driven through the main marked minefield, the convoy broke up and the Egyptians started driving off in all directions, like dogs picking up a scent.

We chased after the tanks heading off to the west and were soon in the front line, bounding over the sand abreast of them as they began to engage unseen targets. As we climbed the crest of a low hill, the armour suddenly stopped as if uncertain what to do next. Behind us the big 155mm howitzers opened up and we could see the shells landing on the lower ground ahead.

The armour turned back on course. Then something unexpected happened. There was a flash and a plume of smoke appeared in the middle of the advancing tanks. The Iraqis were firing back. The shells were coming in at the rate of only one or two a minute but it was enough to make the armour pause. The tanks stopped, unsure of the way through the minefields ahead. This was the scenario envisaged by the designers of the Iraqi defences and their Soviet mentors. The point of the fortifications was to halt attackers, allowing them to be cut to pieces by the artillery dug in behind the lines. Despite the massive bombardment now being directed onto the Iraqi gunlines, the Iraqi artillery was undoubtedly causing the Egyptians some anxiety. Further back, where the convoy had halted, drivers were jumping from their vehicles and digging in. The Iraqi shells seemed to be working their way towards us. Chris and I decided it was time to pull back. We had gone a few hundred metres when we passed a group of command vehicles, festooned with communications wires. Among them was a Humvee with a US liaison time. A shell landed nearby, to the left of the group. Then another exploded to the right. 'We're being bracketed,' one of the Americans yelled. The third shell, though, never arrived. Presumably the gunner had succumbed to the hail of shells pouring down on the Iraqi positions.

We left the battlefield to look for prisoners and came across a group sitting in a bus at the side of the road. It was rather like a park-and-ride operation. The Saudi guards would wait until enough prisoners had showed up to fill the coach, then drive off to Hafr al Battin. The Saudis were unfriendly and would not let the prisoners talk.

When we returned to the battlefield, the Iraqi resistance had crumbled. At one-thirty in the afternoon white flags had begun appearing in the bunkers and hundreds of prisoners had emerged. Despite the efforts of the Iraqi gunners there were no noticeable casualties from the shells. We came across a clinic where five or six men were being treated. One was lying on the ground screaming while a medic picked shrapnel out of his wounds. Another was very badly wounded, probably dying. They had been hurt when they'd dropped a rocket they were loading into a launcher. There were also six casualties from driving over mines, a figure that seemed miraculously low considering the millions of mines scattered in the sand, and the complete disinclination of the Egyptians to stick to swept tracks. We drove nervously back to the road, doggedly following the fattest, deepest tracks we could find.

That evening we all agreed that the war was clearly going to finish the following day. It was imperative to get to Kuwait City. We decided to pool our resources. Chris and I teamed up with David Williams and the *Mail* photographer, Steve

Back, Victor Mallet of the *Financial Times*, Ramsey Smith of the *Daily Mirror* and Stewart Payne of the *Evening Standard*. Next day we set off in convoy, driving east along the al Ruqi frontier road until we found a breach in the Berm. A stream of trucks and tankers was trickling through. After inching along for an hour or so, we reached the Iraqi defensive positions. The story of the war was written in the scorched sand around the supposedly fearsome fortifications. The sand was carpeted with hundreds of white-and-yellow cluster-bomb plastic casings about a metre long. Whole areas hundreds of metres square were pitted with craters from the bomblets. Far from the massive network of berms and bunkers of imagination, the fortifications were amateurish and half-hearted. The first trench line we came across had six bunkers. Most of them had only a strip of corrugated iron and a thin layer of sand dotted with sandbags as overhead cover. Inside the narrow interiors of the better-built bunkers, three or four steps led down two to three metres under the sand, providing some proper protection. But the defences were unmistakably the work of a third-world army. We found a communal bunker smelling strongly of unwashed bodies. There was a tangle of cheap blankets on the floor and some sacking stuck to the wall in an attempt to keep out the cold.

Another bunker, apparently belonging to a commander, was slightly more comfortable with an iron bed, a wrenched-out car seat which served as an armchair and a cheap plastic transistor radio which seemed to be broken. In the shelter next door we found a crude map of the position, inscribed with the words, 'Mohammed is the Prophet of God.'

Compared with the living standards of the attackers, the conditions were wretched. To keep out the rain, cheap green plastic capes the thickness of dustbin liners were used. To wash with, there were bars of hard soap, not the unguents and body shampoos to which the British and American soldiers were addicted. There was no sign of any food apart from a few tins of processed cheese. The abandoned equipment was equally primitive. They communicated with each other on old-fashioned Soviet-issue Bakelite radios. Lying haphazardly around were scores of boxes of rocket-propelled grenades, the main defensive weapon against the allied armour, about as much use against an Abrams tank as an air pistol. There were cases of antique stick grenades and rifle ammunition. By one foxhole a small, rusty mortar with a buckled base plate was lying in the sand. The defenders had not even bothered to set up the weapon's aiming sticks.

Surprisingly, there were no dead bodies visible. Nor could we smell any. It seemed unlikely that the Iraqis would have been willing to expose themselves long enough to bury their dead properly. The piles of excrement in some of the trenches suggested they were too frightened to venture beyond the safety of the bunker to take a crap. But few of the bunkers seemed to have suffered direct hits from allied bombs, although an ammunition dump had been destroyed. Mercifully it seemed that the sound and fury of the allied bombardment had not been matched by an equally spectacular toll in Iraqi lives.

By now we had met up with a Saudi armoured battalion which was engaged in flushing out the remaining defenders. The method was simple. The tanks would drive up to a bunker and fire a burst from the turret-mounted machine gun over the position. This was the signal for the Iraqis to scramble up from their foxholes, waving white flags. A fleet of buses following the advance waited to pick them up. Some of the prisoners threw themselves at the feet of their captors, or pressed around the officers, offering information about the whereabouts of positions. A few were aloof. But most of them had the blank-faced zombie look of the utterly exhausted. Among their number was a twenty-eight-year-old lieutenant from Baghdad. He was short, slim and looked like a clerk. It turned out that before being forced into the

army two months previously, he had worked as an account-
ant and he gripped under his arm a brown plastic attaché
case, a comforting relic of his peacetime existence. The lieutenant was relieved that the ordeal was over and could even
manage a little optimism. He spoke in English in a low,
fervent voice. 'With God's will Saddam Hussein will be
removed and God will give the people of Iraq what they
need, not what they have received from this man. There are
a tremendous amount of people who want him to go but
they can't say so because of his bloody ways. He controls
everything. He is the Godfather of the whole thing. He
wants to own everything in this world. The only ones who
could remove him are the army because the people of Iraq
do not have the means. If it happens it will be through the
army.'

In the early afternoon the Kuwaiti advance met up with the
Saudis about sixty kilometres from the city. Hundreds of
tanks and APCs, with engines rumbling and national flags
streaming in the stiff breeze, stood on the gravel plain awaiting the signal to move. Ahead of us, an A10 twisted and
climbed, positioning itself to swoop on its target. Then it
dived and a thick column of white smoke rose from the
dunes.

   Suddenly the Kuwaitis were off! It was an epic sight. They
swept forward in a great line a kilometre across, the crewmen hunched on their turrets, *keffiyehs* wrapped around
their heads to protect them from the stinging, sand-laden
wind. They were laughing and shouting, and waving victory
signs to us as we cruised alongside them. From time to time
the gunners opened up, although there was no sign of any
Iraqi resistance, or indeed of any Iraqis. The chance to be
able to claim that they had fired their weapons in anger was
not going to be denied them. As we approached the Iraqi
fortifications around Jahra, the bulldozers moved to the

front of the line, punching holes in the sand walls for the columns to race through.

Here the defences were bigger – serious constructions of concrete and steel – but most of them had been smashed to rubble by the allied bombardment. The Ali al-Salam airbase nearby had taken a real pounding. The terminal building had been caved in by the bombs so that the roof now sagged forlornly down to floor level. Near the airbase we came across two terrified Iraqi soldiers lying on the ground. A Kuwaiti jeep drove up and a man jumped down holding a captured Kalashnikov that jabbed in the direction of the Iraqis. While shouting abuse about Saddam, he ordered them up from the sand and made them kneel.

For a moment it seemed that we were about to witness a summary execution. The Iraqis thought so too. Then the Kuwaiti turned back to the jeep and rummaged in the front. He produced a bottle of mineral water, pulled off the top and handed it to one of the prisoners. Limp with relief, the pair were led away.

Dusk was falling fast. The charge across the sands was over. Behind the leading tanks, the rest of the Kuwaiti column had caught up. The long, liquid river of headlights stretched back into the desert. It was time for evening prayers. The crewmen climbed down from their vehicles and bowed towards Mecca to give thanks for their bloodless victory. Looking south, we could see the outskirts of the city illuminated by a huge orange canopy of flickering light from the burning oil installations.

CHAPTER NINE

At first light, after a few hours of jerky, exhausted sleep wedged upright in the front of the Toyota, we set off again towards the city. The Kuwaitis were still unconscious, sprawled under the hulls of their vehicles. As we drove slowly around, trying to find the road, small groups of men emerged from the desert: Iraqis trying to find someone who would allow them to give themselves up. The novelty of taking Iraqi surrenders had long worn off. We despatched them in the direction of the Kuwaitis.

The way into the city was blocked by a cluster of American tanks. It was the Tiger Brigade, just waking up. The sentries advised us not to continue as it was not certain that the road was clear and there were reports that snipers, maybe Palestinian, were shooting at vehicles. The air was foul with the stench from a dead donkey. Another donkey was grazing in the reservation dividing the two carriageways. The reservation was almost certainly mined. We looked on as he shuffled gently forwards and munched stoically away, expecting to see him explode at any moment. Eventually someone threw stones and he reluctantly shifted back onto the road. The door of the command vehicle opened and Tiger Brigade's commander emerged and began stripping off his clothes. He seemed elated and chatted cheerfully as he put on a clean shirt. There had been a bit of fighting, he said. A few insanely brave Iraqi tanks had insisted on firing back and been instantly destroyed. Mostly it had been a question of shooting up abandoned armour.

The real destruction had been a few kilometres down the road where a huge convoy of Iraqi vehicles had been caught fleeing the city. 'The bodies are stacked up like cordwood,' he said. It was at a place called Mutla Ridge.

The Kuwaitis had roused themselves and were beginning to form up behind the Americans ready for the triumphal entry into the city. It took several hours before the column was in place. The Americans dropped away. It was the Kuwaitis' show. Shortly before noon, in a great clanking of tracks, grinding of gears and revving of engines, the cavalcade began rolling forward. Despite the hour it was still not light. The sky was grey, shading into a sinister yellow, and a dirty rain was falling. As we approached the outskirts of town, Kuwait City looked like one imagines Halifax to have been, say in November in 1890. In the distance clouds of filth were pumping into the sky from the sabotaged wellheads and refineries. But the apocalyptic weather could do nothing to blot out the ecstatic joy of a people tasting salvation from life under Saddam Hussein.

It was like the collective awakening from a nightmare. As we reached the suburbs the motorway was suddenly lined with men, women and children, all laughing and crying. Soldiers leaped out from the rumbling column to embrace family members and friends, the noise of the tank tracks was overlaid by the din of automatic fire as the soldiers riding the hulls opened up with rifles and machine guns in a fusillade of joy. When we passed through the working-class area of Sulabiya, children rushed over to us shouting, 'Thank you, thank you.' And old men stood at the side of the road, crying with relief.

However, the real victors, kept at the city gates out of consideration for Arab political sensibilities, were being denied the celebrations.

At one point the procession passed a group of US Marines

lined up in front of a giant stars-and-stripes which streamed out against the bleak grey sky, creating a tableau as dramatic as the famous photograph of the Marines raising the flag in Iwo Jima. The Kuwaitis jumped off their vehicles and ran over to hug them.

As the column approached the city centre, the endless line of armour and trucks was infiltrated by civilian cars. Everyone was waving the green, white, red and black national flag; portraits of the Emir and the Crown Prince had appeared from nowhere and were displayed in the back windows. All along the route lay evidence of the destructiveness of the occupation and of the force that had been used to end it. The road we were travelling on had been one of the Iraqi escape routes and every few metres we passed the browned and blackened hulls of burned-out T72s and T54s. On the right-hand side of the freeway was a hangar-sized luxury car showroom which the Iraqis had virtually demolished by shellfire, after removing the loot to Baghdad.

Downtown, the big hotels were scorched and wrecked. In the new parliament building on the corniche, virtually every window was broken. The beach had been disfigured with barbed wire, trenches and minefields. The boats down at the marina were sieved with holes. Their masts and spars had been snapped off.

It was if a huge army of delinquents had gone on the rampage: the destructiveness was pointlessly malevolent, like that of a vandal spraying obscenities on a statue. The Iraqi actions seemed a bellow of inadequacy, an inarticulate venting of a deep feeling of inferiority. There was something particularly pathetic about the way they had gone around changing the street signs. All over the city they had painted out the Kuwaiti name for a street and substituted an Iraqi one. So that, say 'Adnan al Mukhtar Street', commemorating an al Sabah Emir of old, became with slavish unoriginality 'Saddam Street', or – to introduce a little variety – 'al Rasheed Street'. A few ceramic portraits of Saddam had been erected at intersections but the hateful features were already obliterated by machine-gun bullets. The only other contribution to the townscape made by the Iraqis was the checkpoints.

These were small, crude constructions of corrugated iron and concrete-filled oil barrels. One could easily imagine the guard, slouching forward, cigarette burning, Kalashnikov hung sloppily over shoulder, hand extended insolently for passport, ID card, papers. The tawdry predictability of the Iraqis filled one with disgust, and with foreboding about the stories we were about to hear – which were not long in coming. We decided to set up camp at the British Embassy down near the waterfront. The building was barred and bolted and a mortar trench had been dug in the car park. From the roof, the flag hung limp and stained grey by oily soot.

Within a few minutes of our presence, Kuwaitis, Filipinos, Indians and Sri Lankans who had stayed on arrived eager to shake hands with the Brits – even though, as we explained, we had played no part in the Liberation. Among them was Dr Jafer Mohammed who worked as the chief of preventative medicine at the Ministry of Health. 'It was like living in a concentration camp,' he said.

Why did he stay when so many had fled? He shrugged his shoulders. 'If everyone leaves what is there to fight for? It's my country. I have no other place to go. We didn't leave, because we wanted to prove to the coalition countries that we were a real country.'

A woman turned up looking for something to wave. 'We need an American flag,' she said. 'We need the flags of France, Britain and Israel too.'

People began telling stories of the atrocities. There was an ice rink nearby that had been used as a giant morgue by the Iraqis, they said. David Williams, Victor Mallet and I found a guide and set off to examine it.

The front door was broken and the inside vandalised.

Wires were trailing everywhere. We had been warned to expect booby traps so we lobbed a few bricks through the entrance to trigger any devices. Nothing happened so we stepped carefully inside. The rink was as it had been described. The ice had melted leaving the concrete floor exposed. There were red marks on the floor. The place stank, but did it stink of dead bodies? One had got fairly used to that smell over the years. There was a cafeteria in the corner, full of rotting food which could have been responsible for the familiar nauseating stench. It seemed unlikely that the red stains were blood, as our guides maintained, which would surely have drained away with the melting ice. They looked more like rust. But our companions, two men who had stayed with their families throughout the occupation, were insistent.

One of them, Faisal, had been directed to the ice rink two months before when searching for friends who had disappeared. 'I went there and saw the dead bodies. There were more than two hundred. There were men and women aged between sixteen and thirty. They had their clothes on. They were lying about in disorder. They had all been shot in the head. Some were without eyes, some without ears.' Whether or not the Iraqis allowed people in to identify the dead depended on their mood, he said. Those wanting to remove a body were told they would first have to obtain a death certificate from Baghdad. Faisal said the ice rink had been out of use since the city lost its electricity supply on 17 February. Later, another Kuwaiti told us the story was false and that the skating rink had been out of order since the first week of the occupation.

Faisal's companion, Musa, recounted another story about his cousin Walid. One day some Iraqi soldiers working on a tip-off from a Palestinian had turned up at the house and arrested Walid, claiming he was in possession of a gun and was a member of the resistance. Later they returned to the house asking for 30,000 dinars to release him. The family parted with 10,000 dinars. A week later his body had been dumped outside the house. 'They cut off his penis and cut his eyes out and drilled holes in his hands. They left him in front of the door.'

Chasing evidence of atrocities is a depressing business. True though the stories sounded, they were still only stories. Our guides told us of a cemetery, at Rigga on the outskirts of the city, where the Iraqis' victims were buried. When we arrived there a grisly interment was in progress. A young boy and a very old man were assisting the custodian of the graveyard to bury some dead Iraqis.

The bodies were being tumbled haphazardly into the pit. God knows what had happened to them. The buttocks and back of one corpse were completely burned away. The arm and side of another were like charcoal. Ali, the custodian, was a plump man with an Islamic beard who asked us if we wanted to take photographs. The little boy leaned down and started tugging at the bodies so that we could see their faces. They seemed disappointed when we politely refused the offer.

As the sexton's men began shovelling sand onto the bodies, he took us to the other side of the cemetery where there was a row of long, freshly dug graves. There were thirty-eight of them and each contained four bodies. The corpses had been brought there from the hospitals where they had been dumped by the Iraqis. Or by relatives who found them in the streets. 'Most of them were shot,' Ali explained. 'They had drill marks in their hands and burns from electric shocks.' Some of them were women.

There was one more call to make. At the Adan hospital a few kilometres down the road, any lingering doubts about the essential truth of the Kuwaitis' accusations disappeared.

There in the morgue drawers were the Iraqis' last victims: three Kuwaiti men shot in the side of the head, the back of the head and the heart, respectively. And an Egyptian man shot dead at his home two days before.

In one of the offices I came across a tall, distinguished-looking Egyptian doctor. He looked distracted, with that deceptive nonchalance sometimes to be found in the recently bereaved. He told me his wife had been killed in an allied air attack three weeks before. She was staying in a hostel in the hospital grounds, thinking it would be safer than home, when it was hit by rockets. 'They said it was an accident but it wasn't. They knew what they were doing. We later discovered that the Iraqis had been using the hospital as an ammunition store.' While we were talking, a nurse stuck her head round the door. Could the doctor come quickly? We hurried along the corridor to a casualty ward where a young Saudi soldier was laid out on a stretcher. In the midst of the celebrations that were going on all over the city, he had stepped on, or driven over, a mine. The explosion had broken his left leg and blown open his lower stomach. He was barely conscious and breathing in desperate, short gulps. As I looked on, ashamed of my inability to help, the colour seemed to drain out of him so that his brown skin turned to the colour of clay. The breathing grew harsher and more frantic. Then it stopped. The Egyptian doctor began pounding his chest but it was no use. I stole away.

The road back to the city was jammed with civilian cars: the ubiquitous Chevrolet Caprice Classics packed with children, all hooting and shouting, ear-jarring Arabic pop music pouring from the cassette players. Nearly every young man seemed to have got his hands on a weapon and was spraying automatic fire into the air or, as often as not, at a haphazard angle that threatened everyone around.

The celebrations were to go on for days, creating huge jams that clogged the traffic on the corniche for four or five hours every evening. It seemed a mindless and inappropriate way to mark the event. The natural thought was that people would have grown to detest the sound of gunfire, and never want to hear it again, certainly not want to associate the noise with happiness. Yet night after night, following the

Liberation, the skies were red with tracer fire as the rejoicing went on – prompting the observation that many more bullets were fired celebrating the Liberation of Kuwait than were ever fired defending it.

The Kuwaitis and the Asians were extravagant in their gratitude. As our camp outside the Consulate grew, so did the pile of offerings. Bottles of whisky and cans of beer, their sale forbidden under normal Kuwaiti law, appeared. Families offered journalists the run of their homes. Victor and I decided to try and find a place in the International Hotel, which was rumoured to have opened its doors. It had previously been some sort of Iraqi headquarters, whether for soldiers or functionaries, or both, was not clear. By the time we got there the place had already been colonised by the TV networks, and by teams of journalists taken to the city on bus and plane by the Saudi authorities – our old friends from the JIB. There was no electricity or running water. Out of the corridors and lobbies swam the half-recognisable forms of colleagues picking their way through the gloom with torches. Having been evicted from a succession of places, we eventually found a room where I fell into bed and a coma-like sleep. The rhythm of driving over the rippling desert stayed in my head: I dreamed I was a journalistic Flying Dutchman, chained to the wheel of a Toyota Land Cruiser, doomed to roam the endless sands for ever.

The following morning when we went downstairs, food seemed to be out of the question. We drove back to the Embassy. The colleagues had got themselves organised. In the courtyard in front of the Consulate building, breakfast was cooking on a couple of primus stoves. Steve Back was taking orders for tea or coffee. The satellite phone, set up the day before, was now wired into the mains, thus removing the necessity for the generator. A long shelf along one of the walls was stacked with cans of corned beef, sardines, tuna, baked beans and condensed milk brought with us from

Hafr al Battin. As the day progressed the stores were augmented with supplies bartered locally, notably a case of Russian vodka.

After fortifying ourselves, Victor and I set out to see if any start had been made on clearing up the mess left by the Iraqis. We drove out of town heading south towards a huge cloud of smoke and flame coiling up from the Shweibah refinery thirty kilometres away. As we approached we tried to find suitable words to match the scene. Journalese, so often employed in boosting the unremarkable, is ill-suited to describing the truly spectacular. Victor struggled with an image involving Brueghel. We gave up. It was a very big fire. The firemen at the Ahmadi refinery next door were less impressed, however. It was dramatic but harmless, they said, and rather than tackling it they were going to let it burn itself out. The chief safety engineer at the plant said Iraqi vandalism, and allied bombing to stem the flow of oil into the Gulf after Saddam began to pollute it, had caused only twenty per cent damage. The refineries would be ready for action again within six months. A much bigger problem was the six hundred or so well fires burning all over the country.

The firemen were a mixture of Kuwaitis and Palestinians. During the occupation they had all worked on under an Iraqi team. They had a laugh recalling the ignorance of their temporary bosses. Together they exuded the strong camaraderie common to fire-fighters. They were proud of having stayed on, believing they had saved the refinery from suffering worse damage. The Palestinians may not have suspected, then, that the act of carrying on working would later be considered proof of a lack of loyalty by the Kuwaiti authorities when it began its campaign to drive them out. But they knew that life was about to become very uncomfortable.

As we left we asked if we could buy some petrol, it being unobtainable in Kuwait City. Two of the Palestinians drove with us down to the plant. We parked the cars. One of them walked over and detached a rubber hose from the indecipherable tangle of pipes and valves, and stuck it into the tank. As he filled up our spare petrol cans he talked. As always with Palestinians, we spoke about the place he had originally hailed from, a village on the West Bank. But whatever the Palestinians in Jordan, the West Bank and Gaza may have thought about Saddam, he said, everyone here knew he was bad news. He spoke bitterly. 'After this, forget Palestine. Saddam has killed Palestine. Him and Yasser Arafat.'

Times, he and his mate both agreed, were going to get rough. Already we had heard numerous stories of Palestinians collaborating with the Iraqis, how they'd pointed out the homes of members of the security forces and the resistance, and had looted shops and homes. It was hard to know how much credence to give them. Some of them must have been true. But after pursuing the subject later on several trips back to Kuwait, I remain unconvinced that anything more than a small minority ever gave active help to the invaders.

Victor wanted to see the airport, particularly the wreckage of the British Airways 747 which he had flown in on just as the Iraqis reached the city seven months before. As we approached, the sky darkened. Within a few minutes a freak nightfall had descended. At one o'clock in the afternoon all the cars were driving with full headlights. Already aircraft were arriving. An RAF Hercules made the first flight.

When we got back to the Embassy a dramatic scene was in progress. A Chinook helicopter was hovering above the building, its actions avidly recorded by several TV crews below. A rope was let down and a number of men descended onto the roof.

Shortly afterwards we heard the sound of explosions from inside. 'Don't worry,' said a soldier on the door. 'They're just clearing the place of any booby traps.' Five months later the damage from the Special Boat Squadron's visit was still visible in the Embassy entrance hall.

A little afterwards the Chinook returned with the

ambassador on board. Mr Michael Weston forsook sliding down a rope and alighted in the car park instead. Heavy drops of rain began to fall, laden with soot and oil. The hooting on the corniche did little to lift the spirits. The vodka helped. Most of us had been on the road more or less continuously. It was time to go home. The *Telegraph* was anxious to know what was happening in Southern Iraq, however. The border was only ninety minutes up the road, or at least it had been in normal times.

The following day I set out with Victor and David. So far we had not been north of the city. As we left town heading towards Jahra and Abdalli, we passed a number of burnt out vehicles. Some of them still had corpses lying by the side of them, or stuck inside. It was a Friday, and Kuwaiti sightseers were out in force. Videos whirring, they were cruising the freeway looking for particularly spectacular examples of destruction. The main attraction was a big truck, Soviet by the look of it, slewed to one side of the road. It appeared to have been hit by a rocket. In the cab the corpse of the driver sat upright behind the wheel. His body had shrunk in the flames and his teeth grimaced through the incinerated flesh. One arm was thrown up in a histrionic pose, as if seeking to ward off the incoming missile. On the floor was another corpse, dry and brown, like a mummy. There were two more on the back. Another one or two at the side.

This was just the beginning. As we drove on we saw more and more devastated vehicles. Then we passed under a bridge. The road ahead was impassable. It was choked with tanks, trucks, school-buses, fire-engines, pick-up trucks, looted luxury cars, motorcycles: anything that could be made to move, anything that would get the Iraqis out of the city and away from the advancing army. Suddenly we remembered the words of the Tiger Brigade colonel. *They were stacked up like cordwood.* The jam of burnt and smashed-up vehicles was about five kilometres long.

The story seemed to be that the escaping troops had found

143

their way blocked by American troops and had tried to fight their way through. As the massive convoy backed up behind, it was attacked from the air with rockets and cluster bombs.

The result was a massacre. Many of the vehicles were undamaged by fire but had been wrecked as the drivers smashed into each other in the frenzy to get off the road. One Iraqi had tried to drive his tank over the concrete barrier in the middle of the road. The T55 tank now stood balanced crazily, one track mounted on the top of the metre-high divider. The desert on the eastern side of the road, to the right of the direction the Iraqis were heading, was cluttered to a width of a kilometre with abandoned or destroyed vehicles. We drove in amongst the wreckage. Already there were plenty of British and American looters in evidence, stepping over the corpses lying around untidily to rummage inside the vehicles for souvenirs.

It seemed unlikely there would be much of great value. Even at the last moment, with nemesis arriving at high speed, the Iraqis themselves had still made time to loot. Their idea of what was valuable filled one with pity. Their booty spilled out of the back of the vans and the pick-up trucks: big, old-fashioned televisions; blankets, hundreds of blankets; cheap clothes; even tennis balls. Some of the bodies had been taken away but there were still too many to count. Some had been covered over. They were poor-looking, unshaven, and their uniforms were dirty. You could not see in their pathetic dead faces, on which the flies were now settling, the killers and torturers described by the Kuwaitis. And in all probability these were not the same men. The guilty, like the Mukhabarat spiv who had rapidly vacated our hotel room, had escaped the holocaust – ordered out of Kuwait City a day ahead of the army by their benevolent and appreciative boss. The dead were literally cannon fodder. First for Saddam who had pushed them into the front line in a conflict he could never win. Then for the

American tank crews and pilots, some perhaps anxious to experience the thrill of killing before it was all over.

The ground was covered with unexploded ordnance. We picked a way through, our tyres frequently bumping over mortar bombs and rocket-propelled grenades. The scavenging troops had painted their names and the names of their units on some of the wrecked vehicles. It seemed a strange thing to do. How could anyone want to be associated with this carnage? Eventually after a detour through the sand we arrived at the top of Mutla Ridge. The highway ahead was covered with razor-sharp shrapnel. Within ten minutes we had a punctured tyre. The spare was flat. A passing British jeep took the tyres and David off to a workshop to repair them.

It was late by the time we set off again. On the road we passed small groups of Arabs, walking in the opposite direction. Some had a few possessions, tied to a stick like Dick Whittington's and carried over a shoulder, but most of them had nothing at all. We stopped to talk to four men wearing tattered *gelabiyas* and broken-down sandals. They were Egyptians who had walked all the way from Basra where they said soldiers were shooting their countrymen of whom twenty had been killed in the last five days. One of them described seeing an Iraqi soldier walk into a shopping centre in Basra, fire his rifle in the air, then order all the Egyptians to flee for their lives. Rather belatedly, it seemed that the Iraqis were going to punish Egyptian nationals for their government's decision to side with the allies. Our four had no food apart from an MRE given to them by an American soldier and a bottle of water. We gave them chocolate bars, cigarettes and water and went on our way.

At the frontier the big reinforced-concrete border-post that used to stand there was now a pile of rubble and steel rods, demolished by the Iraqis, presumably because it was unnecessary to have a customs gateway to the nineteenth province. A BBC TV crew was hanging about at the side of the road looking anxious. Brian Barron, the correspondent, explained that they had just driven up the road to Sawfan where they had encountered an Iraqi checkpoint. The soldiers manning it, who had been friendly earlier in the day, had turned nasty and stolen the camera. The crew were now hoping that the American soldiers nearby would go and get it back. We drove, timorously, a few hundred metres up the road towards Safwan. The checkpoint was still there. The afternoon was wearing on. There seemed little point in continuing into Southern Iraq. We turned back to Kuwait City. The BBC's translator asked if we minded giving a lift to his cousin, who had just arrived at the frontier from Basra.

His name was Abdullah al Badran and he was a twenty-four-year-old student from Kuwait City. He had gone to Basra to buy food. As we drove along he calmly recounted the events in the city in the past few days. The place was in a state of anarchy. Baath party officials had fled and the army was breaking up and deserting in droves. He described a scene, incredible before the war, that had taken place at nine o'clock the morning before. A tank had driven into one of the main squares of the city and fired three rounds through a portrait of Saddam positioned next to the Baath party headquarters. 'The people cheered. They shouted "Saddam is finished. All the army are dead."' The other tanks standing around nearby had done nothing to intervene and soldiers had joined in the demonstration. 'They were all shooting in the air and saying they don't like Saddam. . . .'

He said also that the government had disappeared; that soldiers were stripping off their uniforms, abandoning their weapons and leaving.

This was extraordinary and heartening news. One could imagine the satisfaction of the soldier who'd had the pleasure of sending a 120mm shell crashing through the grinning, hateful features of the tyrant. But such an act would have taken a considerable effort of that same soldier's will. If he was young, Saddam's face would have been a constant motif

146

throughout his life. He would have seen scores of portraits from the bus on the way to school and there would have been more waiting for him when he arrived: in hall, class-room, gym. Whenever he went for a Pepsi with a friend in the evening, the President would have been looking down on him from behind the café till. And there, too, smiling from the wall of his parents' home when he returned to go to bed. How much more he would have loved to have fired at the real thing!

We raced back to Kuwait City to file our stories, which seemed to be the first reports of trouble in the South. On Sunday we returned to the border, determined to try and get into Basra. On the way up we encountered a stream of refugees who enlarged on the story of the revolt. On Satur-day, they said, a crowd had broken into the al Haritha jail in the city – killing the governor and freeing 2,000 prisoners. Any Baathis who had not already fled were being hunted down and killed. The demonstrators in the streets were now calling for an Islamic regime, they were shouting for Saddam to be overthrown and for Mohammed Bakr, a Shia cleric, leader of the Supreme Assembly of the Islamic Revolution, now living in exile in Iran, to replace him.

One man said that there'd been hundreds of soldiers in the streets. 'They were laughing,' he said. But a Jordanian refugee spoke of fighting between soldiers and civilians in which many were killed.

When we reached Abdalli, the road leading the short dis-tance to Safwan on the Iraqi side was blocked by American troops. A short distance away, General Schwarzkopf was signing the cease-fire agreement with a party of Iraqi gen-erals. A large group of journalists had assembled, some concerned with the signing ceremony, some with trying to get to Basra. Going to Basra was clearly going to be dodgy. From the optimistic point of view, the Islamic rebels might welcome us – eager to get some publicity for their cause. On the other hand, we had come from the allied side, from

147

the people who had just been dropping bombs on them. Furthermore it was by no means clear who controlled the area around Basra.

Suddenly the road was open again and a soldier was waving us through, standing in the middle of the track like a traffic policeman directing those for the signing ceremony this way, those for Basra that way. Some of the people in our car were still wearing uniform. I pulled over to the side while my companions rapidly pulled off their fatigues and stuffed them into a rucksack which we dumped behind a tree. We were in the middle of a convoy of fifteen or sixteen cars. As we drove on into Iraq we felt a mounting sense of unease. On either side of the road stood ragged Iraqi soldiers who looked at us with complete amazement. We hung out of the windows frantically waving and smiling, desperate not to show the slightest hostile intent. The soldiers looked puzzled and smiled warily back. The road was surprisingly undamaged, but it was clear that the war had hit the local people hard. We saw women collecting water from puddles. Everyone looked dirty and undernourished. There were hardly any vehicles on the road, and those we saw were battered and chugging feebly along.

The most alarming sight was the portraits. Whatever destruction was being done to the Saddam icons in Basra, they were intact here. We passed a particularly grotesque example opposite an army barracks, in which the dictator was smiling beatifically, surrounded by doves of peace. After that we crossed a railway line. Off to the east there seemed to be an industrial area. Was this the outskirts of the city? The cars up ahead slowed down, then stopped. We had hit a roadblock. The occupants of the vehicle two in front seemed to be in some difficulty. And the soldiers were shouting and waving their rifles. I spoke to one of them who was standing nearby. 'Don't go any further,' he said. 'Things are no good.' He warned that there were Republican Guard units further up the road and claimed that the Baath party were still in power in Basra.

We pulled back, reluctant to leave until our colleagues extricated themselves from the contretemps. Eventually they too returned. But the front half of the convoy had sailed through the roadblock before the soldiers had had time to realise what was going on and was on its way to Basra. We learned later that they had all been arrested by government troops a few kilometres further on and were taken to Baghdad before being released.

The following day we returned to the border again. The straggle of refugees on the road confirmed the Islamic nature of the uprising, which appeared to have spread to several other cities in the South including the Shiite holy city of Najjaf. They described scenes reminiscent of the early days of the Iranian revolution, with demonstrators carrying pictures of Islam Ali, the deposed and murdered seventh century Caliph and founding father of Shi'ism.

But already it seemed that Saddam was preparing to fight back. A Kuwaiti soldier attached to the US forces had spent the morning debriefing refugees. They'd told him that the Republican Guard were lined up on one side of Basra and controlled the roads in and out of the city. 'They have been firing with tanks at houses and totally destroying them,' he reported. There were stories that a Republican Guard unit had moved in to the crush a Shiite revolt led by the fundamentalist Dawa party in the town of Zubeir, near Basra. It was already clear from talking to the American soldiers that, despite pleas from the rebels, they had no intention of going to their aid.

The allies had decided that the war was over. So for the moment did I. The following day I set out for Dhahran. Already the roads were choked with American troops flooding south.

CHAPTER TEN

On a hot May morning two months after leaving the Gulf, I found myself back in the Middle East, in Basra's main square, looking at a giant frame which had once held a portrait of Saddam Hussein. It was through this picture that the anonymous tank-gunner had fired three rounds in the brief, heady days of the uprising. The town bore the marks of vicious fighting: bullet-pocked and smoke-scorched buildings, walls demolished by shellfire. Already, though, the official icon painters had been busy and like some ineradicable stain, Saddam's image was reappearing around town. Significantly the artists had chosen to depict him in a gentler light. Instead of the usual warrior or statesman image he was portrayed as an avuncular figure wearing a white pork-pie hat, a white polo shirt, shades and a diffident grin. In a dictatorship like Iraq's such touches clearly had some meaning. For the time being, at least, it seemed that the regime felt it was more expedient to placate than to punish. The peace that had finally settled on the area was a sullen one. The local population seemed to have accepted grudgingly that Saddam was there to stay. The authorities for their part seemed reluctant to provoke them. Basra had an air of laxity that was unthinkable in pre-war days, with the inhabitants imparting opinions that only a few months before could easily have resulted in arrest, torture and death.

We had driven down from Baghdad that morning accompanied by two minders from the Ministry of Information.

150

Judging by the war damage we saw on the way, the boasts concerning the precision of smart weaponry seemed justified. In Baghdad itself the skyline was more or less as I remembered it. Driving around town, one saw spectacular examples of destruction – with whole buildings dropped where they stood as if part of some enormous urban renewal project. But the houses, offices and shops around were usually virtually untouched. The most dramatic example of the bomber's art was the Amariyah shelter in a suburb of the city – where more than 700 Iraqis, mainly women and children, were killed by an American bomb. From the outside the building looked intact. Standing inside, you gazed up at a neat hole in the roof where the bomb had smashed through three metres of steel-reinforced concrete, penetrated a floor below and exploded. It was a bull's-eye. It was a pity the allied Intelligence had not been so accurate. In the middle-class streets outside nearly every villa displayed a black flag inscribed with the names of the household's victims. Sometimes there were five or six names.

It was the same story with the factories and power plants we passed on the long journey south. From the outside they looked undamaged. But there was no smoke issuing from the chimneys, no sign of activity round about, and wouldn't be until their wrecked control rooms were repaired. The further south we went the more the population was suffering. The devastation had plunged the country firmly into the lower reaches of the third world. As we passed through al Amarah we saw huge crowds of women queueing up to buy gas cylinders which they carried away on their heads. On the banks of the Tigris, in the shadow of the wrecked bridges, men sat fishing; others walked along the bank carrying the paltry catch to their flimsy reed-homes among the palm trees.

This was oil-rich Iraq, with the potential to make its citizens if not as rich as the bloated Kuwaitis next door, prosperous, comfortable and well-provided for. Instead the money

151

had been squandered on weapons that didn't work, at least not against a proper army, though they were fine for crushing the citizens at home.

The first thing you noticed on reaching Basra was the smell, the stench of the sewage lying in pools at the side of the road, where it had backed up after the pumps failed. There were puddles of water everywhere. Allied bombing had broken many of the mains, and others had been smashed by the locals trying to get water after the taps failed. Down in the souk the shops were full of goods: tins of fish from Iran; beer from Holland; rice from India; cigarettes from Jordan. They began to appear after the government abandoned its socialist practices and allowed unbridled free trade in an attempt to fill bellies. The problem was that no one had any money to spend. Milk and meat had virtually disappeared from most people's diets. The United Nations Children's Fund estimated that eight per cent of children under one year of age in Basra were suffering from malnutrition, and that 100,000 children nationwide were threatened. Officials spoke of a vicious circle where the undernourished were further weakened by diarrhoea caused by bad water and exposure to diseases like cholera and typhoid fever.

In the souk we came across a young man selling cigarettes. He said he was twenty-five years old and had deserted from the army earlier that month. He was angry with the allies, but for interesting reasons. 'Why did you not go all the way to Baghdad?' he demanded. One day, he said firmly, Iraq would break up and there would be a separated southern Shiite state.

A young student approached me as I was leaving and told me that a man had recently been shot dead in the souk for insulting Saddam. This candour was unthinkable before the war.

Other things remained unchanged, however. Our minders had arranged for us to meet the new city governor, General Latif Hammoud, who took charge of the city at the end of the war and had been decorated by Saddam for his part in the 'thirty-fold aggression' as the official propagandists had designated the war. He was the model of a Baath stalwart, with his moustache, well-pressed olive green uniform and absurdly pompous manner. He sat bolt upright at his desk, sweat from the TV lights glistening on his pudgy face, and began to lie. The events of March, he said, were not an uprising but the action of Iranian infiltrators and saboteurs. 'Iraqis strongly love their leader President Saddam Hussein because he has become an integral part of their history. Any attempt to detach the leader from his people will be futile. I have a piece of advice to all these forces to stop their attempts because they will fail.' It was a lesson that the local people seemed to have taken to heart.

The uprisings had shaken the regime into announcing widespread political reforms, including the abolition of the Baath Revolutionary Command Council and its replacement with government by an elected president, a parliament and an executive with complete separation of powers. Political parties were to be legalised and the press set free. If these promises were taken seriously then the Baath party was preparing to share power. But no one believed this. Iraqis looked blankly when asked what they thought about the proposed changes.

Much was made of the lively stand of a new paper, *Babil*. Its claims to independence were tarnished somewhat by the fact that the editor-in-chief was the President's son, Uday Hussein, a convicted murderer. The front office of the newspaper was adorned with the inevitable portait of Saddam, but also with a picture of young Uday. In recent weeks the paper had hosted a seminar at the university at which the subject of the war had been raised. Uday had been asked what Iraq had gained from the war. He replied that if the plan had succeeded Iraq would have controlled the world's largest oil reserves.

The depth of Saddam's failure had done nothing to dilute

the cult of personality. Within a few weeks of the end of the war he had begun appearing again in public. By bribery or coercion the local party managers could still succeed in getting out a respectable crowd to cheer and chant. The nightly TV news carried pictures of his visits to provincial towns. His physique, his movements, had become horribly familiar: the gunslinger's lope, the right arm raised to shoulder height, palm outstretched, the gesture he had invented himself and which was celebrated in the giant bronze statue in the middle of Baghdad. But what did it signify? Was he abstractedly pointing, as if to his achievements? On the other hand, the gesture was reminiscent of the condescending wave of the performer at the end of the show, inviting the audience to applaud themselves. Perhaps, like Hitler's air-clutching and fist-shaking, it meant nothing at all and had merely been invented one day in front of the mirror. The actions of the functionaries lining up to meet Saddam were just as stylised. They kept their eyes demurely lowered, then moved forward to press their lips to his lapels, like pious old women kissing the cardinal's ring.

One day the paper announced that Saddam had been to visit a family in Souk al Jedid, a poor part of Baghdad. He had lodged in the quarter with a relation when he'd arrived from Takrit, a young Baathist thug on the make. Alan Cowell of the *New York Times* and I decided to go and see the family. The minders readily agreed. The al Maharthidi family lived in a crumbling old house, built round a court-yard in which the smells of the lavatory mingled with the neighbours' cooking. Falah al Maharthidi was forty-one but looked sixty. The visit of the *rais* was clearly the most important thing that had ever happened to him. 'It was about seven in the morning,' he said, smiling fondly at the memory. 'My little girl Najam woke me up. She said, "The President is in the street outside!" I rushed out and he was coming through the door. The first thing he said was that the house was very old and gave an order to repair it. Then when he

154

heard that the house belonged to the government, he told me it was now mine.' Before Saddam departed two and a half hours later, Falah had been given back his old job as a gardener at the Ministry of Culture and 2,000 dinars, nearly a year's wages, to buy clothes for his wife and seven children. It was with complete sincerity that Falah said, 'He is a nice man. He is like a brother and a father to me.'

The family proudly produced a brown plastic photograph album that had been presented to them afterwards. If the thirty-fold aggression was a traumatic experience for the Iraqi people it appeared to have had little effect on their leader. The *rais* beamed from the group shot, hands resting lightly on the children's shoulders, slim, fit and confident-looking.

We were intrigued by the lengthiness of the encounter. Two and a half hours seemed considerably more time than was strictly necessary if the intention was merely a photo-opportunity for the local newspapers and TV. What on earth had they talked about? Saddam, Falah said, had shown concern about food prices, which had shot up since the removal of controls from the private sector, and had promised that plans were in hand to bring them down. He asked about the children, and reminisced about the old days when he'd lived in the area. Was any mention made of recent dramatic events? we asked. 'No, no,' said Falah, vigorously shaking his head. 'Not the war, not politics.' In Souk al Jedid, Fawlty Towers' rules clearly applied: When talking to Saddam, you Don't Mention the War.

We asked if the family had offered the President a cup of tea? Indeed they had. And some nice chocolates hygienically wrapped in gold paper. Had he drunk the tea? Falah looked thoughtful. No, he hadn't. But he had eaten one of the chocolates.

Saddam was right to be wary of untested cups of tea. The sort of stunt he'd pulled in Souk al Jedid might win him a bit of local support from hopefuls optimistic that Saddam

Claus might knock on their door one day. But as we travelled around Iraq it became clear that most people hated their leader.

One day we made a trip to Kirkuk, a mixed town of Arabs, Kurds and Turcomans on the edge of Kurdistan. Our activities were heavily circumscribed by a minder from the governor's office. But as we were leaving the market he turned his back. A man we had been previously talking to darted out of the crowd, stuck his head through the car window and hissed, 'You must understand that all the people hate Saddam Hussein very, very, very much.'

A few minutes earlier a courteous old man had followed us out of a café where we had been talking to some Baath party loyalists. 'There are no human rights in Iraq,' he whispered.

'In what way?'

'In every way.'

Neither man was a Kurd, they were both Arabs, probably Sunnis and therefore from the dominant political group. They were prepared to risk their lives to give vent to their feelings. Yet in the days before the war, Western diplomats in Baghdad would often express the opinion that Saddam enjoyed a significant measure of popular support. The Iraqis, they said, recognised the centrifugal forces working on their society and the necessity of a strong man, even a cruel man, to hold its disparate parts together.

This portrayal of Iraqis as a nation of masochists who understood only the club, the bullet, the electrode to the genitals, always struck me as offensively condescending. The official adoration was completely phoney. Only one man in Iraq loved Saddam: himself. The Baathist *apparatchiks* had long ago lost any faith they might have had in their own ideology. The party wasn't a party but a gang, and the members dressed and spoke like gangsters.

In Kirkuk we paid the obligatory visit to the governor's

office. The city boss was Hashim Hassan al Majid. He was the brother of the local government minister Ali, a ruthless figure even by Iraqi standards who had served as the first governor of Kuwait after the invasion. The martial effect of his Baath party uniform was rather spoiled by the thick gold watch, gold chain and diamond-studded rings. He was aloof and hostile. One of the joys of journalism is that one can be offensive to unpleasant people and be fairly sure of getting away with it. In order to get a rise, I asked him if the government had had any second thoughts about the wisdom of the invasion of Kuwait. He rose unerringly to the bait. 'This was not an invasion,' he snapped. 'It was a measure to defend Iraq.' He added defiantly that, 'Kuwait is part of Iraq since eternity.' A colleague asked if the governor was aware that this sentiment was not government policy and that Iraq had renounced its claim to its neighbour. There was a whispered consultation with an aide. The governor cleared his throat. 'We are with the policy of the state, whatever it is,' he said smoothly.

Looking at these men, it seemed obvious that the only reason they were sticking by Saddam was that if he went they would go with him. The boss might be losing his touch a bit, overreaching himself perhaps with the Kuwait blag, but who was there to replace him? Put in a softie and no one knew what might happen. Or rather everyone knew only too well. The first stop-off for rampaging Shiites or Kurds was always the local Baath party office, the first item on the agenda the killing of as many officials as they could lay hands on. Imagine if this spread to Baghdad.

In the meantime the wages were still being paid. The rest of Iraq might go hungry but the torturers, the murderers, the functionaries that kept the engines of terror turning, were guaranteed their place at the trough.

As for the army, the spirit of its officer corps had long ago been broken by the ruthless purging of anyone who showed any sign of dissent or indeed of any great talent. Talent could bring success; success, popularity; popularity, power; power, danger and death. Mediocrity was the best way of staying alive. There was little chance that a coup could be engineered from lower down the ranks, despite the terrible sufferings of the troops. On the whole Iraqi soldiers didn't mutiny, they deserted. On the way back from Kirkuk we passed several truck loads of Republican Guards, the 'élite' Republican Guards of newspaper cliché, whose loyalty was bought with triple pay. Their uniforms were dirty and unbuttoned, they were unshaven, half of them weren't wearing shoes. They looked sullenly at us as we waved and smiled. Nonetheless they, or their comrades, were still capable of a certain efficiency in the domestic violence department. On leaving Kirkuk some of our party, to the fury of their minder, had stumbled on a remarkable scene of devastation in a Kurdish part of town called Shorja. An area 200 metres square had been systematically flattened. Not one stone stood upon another. A passer-by said a thousand people had been killed, mostly civilians. An aid worker told us later that the damage had been done by mortars.

The war had made life for the majority a demeaning scrabble for survival. I came across a man who in better times had worked as a teacher. 'It costs fifty dinars a day to feed my family but I am paid six dinars a day,' he said. In an attempt to make ends meet he was trying to sell scraps of wire wool in the street.

It was the same story in the thieves' market in Baghdad which in its way served as a monument to Saddam's folly. There for ninety pounds you could buy a Breitling Navitimer, official issue to the Iraqi air force with a crest and Arabic inscription on the back to prove it. Once they had been proud possessions, proof of membership of a military élite. At some point they had been sold in their hundreds, presumably to buy food or some other necessity of life. Even though they were on sale at a tenth of the price they go for in London or Paris, the only people who could afford them were journalists and aid workers. It was the same with most of the goods on display. The place was crammed with products looted from the air-conditioned shopping malls of Kuwait. You could buy stereo systems, video cameras, mobile telephones, gold-plated pens, all the accoutrements that the despised Kuwaitis loved. Before the war the Baghdadis used to point to the stolen ware and chuckle. 'Ali Baba,' they would say, making pocket-picking gestures. To the optimistic these goods had looked like the first instalment in the cornucopia that would flow from the invasion. Now they were a reminder of the essential tawdriness of the venture: a smash-and-grab raid disguised as the righting of an injustice.

The hawkers would stand there for hours on end without a bite. Most of the goods were useless in the circumstances. One stallholder's stock consisted of six ping-pong balls and two electric fires. The only people doing business were those selling *laban*, the delicious salty yogurt drink; or sweet, black tea.

Poor Iraq. An old man talked nostalgically of the good old days of Nouri Said and King Faisal, days when there were three meals on the table every day and wars were few and far between. Who could have imagined, as the slow descent into nightmare began with the Quassem coup, that it would ever reach such depths?

For all their sufferings at the allied hands, the Iraqis never treated any of us with anything less than warmth, hospitality and friendliness. While I was in Basra some dust blew into my face, grazing an eyeball. After trying to get it seen to by various Western nurses, I went off to the local teaching hospital. The doctor in charge of the ophthalmic department dropped everything to come and see me. He had trained in Edinburgh and spoke enthusiastically about Britain and Scotland. What had happened had happened between governments, not peoples, he said. I was passed on to

159

another doctor who deftly patched up my eye, handed me some eye-drops and sent me on my way. 'Write good things about Iraq,' I was told as I walked out the door.

The good things in Iraq are the people. Most of the Iraqis outside the government I encountered in my four visits there were good-hearted, well-intentioned and certainly in possession of a much better sense of humour than their Gulf neighbours. Their misfortune was their leaders, a misfortune that was not of their making and which needed suicidal bravery to remedy.

Often when driving through the Iraqi countryside, you see a small child sitting on a donkey, mindlessly flogging it as it trots obediently on its way. Nothing the donkey can do will relieve the beating. He will be hit whether he goes slow or fast. This, I often thought, is what life must be like under Saddam. A beast of burden, under the lash, endlessly.

CHAPTER ELEVEN

A few weeks after leaving Iraq, I returned to Kuwait. I checked into the International Hotel. The place had become a monument to the war. In the lobby the images of the conflict flickered night and day on two television screens that continuously relayed the numerous Gulf War video packages put out by the networks. In the corner there was a display of the hotel furniture that had been wrecked by the occupying Iraqis, and even an exhibition of allied ration-packs.

The city had been cleaned up a bit since I'd last seen it. But there was little sign of large-scale reconstruction. That would have to wait until the Kuwaitis had decided which helots they were going to hire to do the job, and at what price. The businessmen hanging around the hotels waiting for an audience with the relevant official complained that the Kuwaitis had lost none of their taste for hard bargaining, and haggled over every dinar.

In the case of the oil fields, they had to be decisive, however. One day I drove down to the Ahmadi oil area where teams of foreign fire-fighters were dousing and capping some of the 650 or so well-heads vandalised by the Iraqis. The fires had created an infernal landscape of scorched sand and lakes of sticky, black crude. Every few hundred metres, huge tongues of flame licked from the ground and emitted a roaring noise like a jet engine. From the well-heads rose great, coiling columns of smoke, some black, some white, depending on the amount of sulphur in the oil. Every surface was dappled with spots of oily soot.

I found the fire-fighters in a rest-house canteen where they were eating their lunch at eleven a.m. They started their day at four a.m. in an effort to beat the heat. The place had the atmosphere of a cattle-ranch bunkhouse. The oil-men lounged on the veranda in their oil-spattered overalls, chewing tobacco and drinking soft drinks. Some of them had scars from oil burns covering half their faces. Among them was a small, wiry man in red dungarees. Red Adair was seventy-six now but still going out every morning to supervise his team. He spoke in an almost unintelligible Texan accent. However it was clear that he was unimpressed with the Kuwaiti authorities' approach to the problem. His men were still experiencing delays getting visas into the country. He was concerned about the medical facilities.

A little way down the road a British bomb-disposal team was engaged in clearing up the debris of the war. The conflict had left the desert dotted with unexploded bomblets from the cluster bombs and huge caches of ammunition were still being found in the Iraqi positions. The beaches had all been mined and the mines were still claiming victims. The week before two boys had had their legs blown off while playing by the sea near Kuwait City. A government advertising-campaign in the press and on television warning 'don't be another victim of Saddam' seemed to have had little effect and a doctor at the Adan hospital told me that in the month of April, fifteen people had been killed and forty injured. During one recent day eleven victims had been brought in, all children. Two were dead, four required amputations and the others had serious internal bleeding.

The job of the British mine-clearing team, most of them former sappers, was to clear the way to the oil installations so that the fire-fighters could move in to extinguish the blaze or cap the gusher.

Today they were combing the area round an oil-gathering

station that had been flattened by allied fuel air bombs. To the left and right of the desert track, the sand was covered with bomblets, anti-personnel devices, anti-armour devices: all of which would explode at the slightest touch. It made one think back with horror at the risks we had been taking when driving through the Iraqi positions four months before. Many of the bombs were now invisible, covered by the constantly shifting sands, or blended in with the surrounding metal debris. One of the team pointed to some innocuous-looking bits of fabric sticking out of the sand. They were the tails of small M42 bomblets, delivered by an American cluster bomb. The canister contained only thirty grammes of explosive, but it was enough to knock out a jeep or kill anyone who trod on it.

Getting rid of them was going to be a long, laborious and dangerous job. Each cluster-bomb pod contained up to 420 devices. According to the bomb-disposal team, up to half of these might not have exploded. No one knew how many cluster bombs had been dropped. In addition to finding and destroying allied ordnance, the team was blowing up between twenty and twenty-five tonnes of tank, artillery and mortar rounds left behind by the Iraqis and often dangerously unstable due to exposure to the sun.

The overseas specialists had an ambivalent attitude towards the Kuwaitis. On the one hand they were making good money from them. On the other, they were surprised at their total lack of interest in doing anything for themselves that they could pay someone else to do. The French army, which carried out some early beach clearance, had offered before they left to train Kuwaiti soldiers to carry on the work. The offer was declined. The message was that the French could carry on with what they were doing and the government would pay them for it.

The question of how Kuwait was to deal with its manpower problem was one which greatly exercised the government. The one lesson it had taken to heart from the invasion was that it would have to wean itself off its addiction to foreign labour, especially that provided by the Palestinians. Before the war there had been about 650,000 Kuwaiti citizens. They made up only twenty-eight per cent of the population. The war had caused many foreigners to leave. The aim was to scale down their number to around 1.3 million, so that Kuwaitis would make up at least half of the population.

In the government's eyes the Palestinians, and the stateless Arabs known as Bedoon, had shown themselves to be politically unreliable. A decision was taken to drive them out. One means of doing this was the series of martial-law trials of supposed collaborators, most of whom were non-Kuwaitis.

By the time of my return, about three hundred cases had already been heard and a further hundred were expected. So far the courts had handed out twenty-nine death sentences to men and women. I went along to a hearing at the main law courts in Kuwait City. Outside the courtroom I met the father of one of the defendants, a twenty-one-year-old of Palestinian origin called Khaled Fatih, who had been accused of collaborating with the enemy, of robbery and of entering the country without authority. His father was pacing up and down, looking nervous and unhappy. The charges were nonsense, he said. His son had been picked up a few hundred metres from his home by the army on 2 March, a few days after the Liberation. He had done nothing. He was just a high-school student.

A high-school student at twenty-one? I went in to see if I could talk to him. He was sitting in a metal cage with the other defendants, smiling vacantly. He looked about fifteen and had a large head and a cleft palate. When I started speaking, his companions on either side intervened to translate for him, but it was clear that he had no idea who I was or what I was talking about. This man – he seemed more like a harmless child – had been an Iraqi agent?

In the court was one of the defence lawyers, a lady called

Maryam Marafi. She took advantage of the presence of some journalists to deliver a little lecture. 'You are against Kuwait and against the government,' she said. 'We did a lot for the Palestinians. Saddam Hussein taught them how to be criminals.'

The same day the government announced that martial law would be lifted. Khaled's case had been adjourned. It would now be heard by a civil court. Most of the remaining cases, it was expected, would be heard by the state security court. The penal code remained the same: with the crimes of endangering the independence of the country, or of handing over defence secrets, carrying a mandatory death sentence – though this was never actually carried out. It seemed likely that the decision had been prompted by the United States, which had been dismayed at Kuwait's post-liberation disregard for human rights.

It did not matter to the Kuwaitis. They had got their point across. Every Palestinian I spoke to, then and on a subsequent visit, accepted that there was no future for them in the country.

One evening I had dinner in a Palestinian café called al Lydda al Ramleh. The name of the place was a melancholy reminder of the Palestinians' lot. It referred to the Palestinian home towns of the owner and his wife, who had fled them during the Arab-Israel war of 1948. Now most of the clientele were on the move again, though this time it was their Arab brothers who were kicking them out. One of the waiters had come to Kuwait six years before from Tulkaram in the West Bank. He had been a teacher but had lost his job after the invasion. He was worried about his uncle, a man of sixty-one, who had gone off to obtain exit visas for himself and his children two days before and had not come back. When I spoke to an ICRC official about the matter the following day, he said he had probably been detained, then packed off to Jordan. The waiter was planning to return to his own home town. 'At least the Israelis have some respect

165

for human rights,' he said. These sentiments would have amounted to blasphemy only a few months before. The fact they were being uttered now was a measure of the Palestinians' despair.

One young man told me that people would call to him in the street, 'You Palestinians all have Aids. You should carry a government health warning.' This was the least of their problems. The beating and torturing of the early days of the Liberation had now given way to systematic persecution. Palestinians were regularly being arrested and deported – dumped on the Iraqi border where the Iraqis would bus them on to Jordan. Those left behind were left in no doubt that the milch cow that had provided them with jobs, education and a measure of security for many years, was no longer producing. Government employees were told they would not get their old jobs back. And most Kuwaiti employers – there were some honourable exceptions – stopped hiring Palestinians.

The problem of where to go was a serious one. The traditonal refuge of distressed Palestinians, Jordan, was already overflowing with 200,000 former residents of Kuwait who had arrived during the crisis. Egypt had made it plain that it was not interested in having them, even those originating from the Gaza Strip and carrying Egyptian papers. There was nothing for them in Iraq. In these circumstances the lure of the West Bank, under occupation or not, was strong.

Kuwaitis by and large were unsympathetic. 'Maybe five in a hundred Palestinians are good,' a taxi driver told me one day. 'The rest . . .' he spat expressively on the floor. 'When the Iraqis were here the Palestinians would call to my wife and say, "Come over here, I want someone to clean my house." What can you do with these people? Now the Syrians, the Egyptians and Israelis are good. Why do they say the Israelis want to kill the Palestinians? If it was true they would have done it by now.'

The attitude of more educated Kuwaitis outside the ranks

of the left-wing opposition was not dissimilar, though more elegantly expressed. Along with the alleged political unreliability of the Palestinians, they objected to their clannishness and the way they did business. The Palestinians seemed to have few friends in the Western Embassies either. On this count they were paying the price for the behaviour of their cousins in the occupied territories and Jordan.

Most of the Palestinians I spoke to had no faith in Saddam and had never regarded him as an answer to anything. 'He kills his own people,' said one. 'Why should he help us?' But the stereotype had been established: Palestinians were conspiratorial; they kept themselves to themselves; they were too fond of money. It would all have been very familiar to the inhabitants of the Jewish Pale of Settlement in the nineteenth century.

The charge of political unreliability was much harder to make against the Bedoon. These were Arabs, often of Iraqi origin, who frequently had lived and worked in Kuwait for many years, but had never satisfied the country's stringent citizenship requirements and were therefore stateless. The Bedoon formed the backbone of Kuwait's armed services and police force. They had actually put up a fight against the Iraqi invaders on 2 August. Some of them had been captured and taken off to imprisonment in Southern Iraq. When they were freed during the Shia uprising in March, and tried to make their way back across the border to their homes, the authorities refused to allow them back in.

At the time I was there 2,900 Bedoon – men, women and children – were being held at the Abdally refugee camp near the old frontier post. One morning I hired a taxi to take me up there, bluffing my way through five roadblocks where the soldiers' orders were to prevent unauthorised journalists from visiting the camp. The Red Cross workers who supervised the camp had told me in Kuwait City that the inhabitants were either returning soldiers or families who had gone to stay with relations in Southern Iraq during the conflict.

167

The camp was broiling in 120 degree heat and was swept by a stinging, gritty wind. Children in grubby robes wandered about through the guy ropes while their parents sat around listlessly. The inhabitants all claimed to be residents of Kuwait and many had driving licences and bank documents to prove it. But the government was in no hurry to process their claims. Their strategy appeared to be that if the Bedoon were kept there long enough, they would eventually get fed up with the tedium and discomfort of camp life and drift back into Iraq. That was what appeared to be happening. When I returned to Kuwait a month later, the number at the camp had shrunk to about 1,000.

This was one way of dealing with a small section of the Bedoon. But what about the rest? All in all there were perhaps 200,000 in Kuwait, twice the number of remaining Palestinians. The government had given little serious thought to the consequences of kicking them out. They had decided that henceforth all military personnel wearing uniform would have to be Kuwaiti citizens. Previously the armed forces had numbered about 25,000. The British military team advising the government on its future defence strategy recommended that henceforth there should be a minimum strength of 30,000. Raising this number from the ranks of Kuwaiti manhood would mean conscription, a move that would jar unpleasantly with existing social attitudes. Army commanders were even talking about a citizens' army along Swiss or Israeli lines. The idea of pot-bellied middle-aged Kuwaitis struggling into uniforms and setting off for training weekends defied imagination.

There was a constant low grumbling coming from the *diwaniyas* – political salons – of the opposition groups on the subject of the al Sabahs. The main complaints were that the government was dragging its feet in restoring constitutional rule, suspended in 1986. Elections had been announced, but not until October 1992. In the meantime the National Council was recalled, a virtually impotent body that served to drape a thin veil of democracy over the oligarchic form of al Sabahs' rule. The opposition charged that the government was hoping that the council members would be sufficiently well established by the time of the elections to see off their challenge. The critics were a diverse collection, left-wing progressives, merchants, fundamentalists, grouped together into a makeshift alliance that by necessity could only move at the speed of its slowest member.

It was hard to gauge how much support they enjoyed. The al Sabah family had performed disastrously during the run-up to the invasion: failing to read correctly the signals coming from Baghdad; declining to mobilise the army in case it antagonised the Iraqis; running away when the Iraqis invaded anyway. Since their belated return they had behaved with a serene high-handedness, jealously guarding their power, refusing to be hurried into any great show of vigour or efficiency.

Yet virtually every Kuwaiti seemed to accept that there was no alternative to rule by the al Sabahs. It was a question of how *much* power they should be allowed to keep in their hands. Few Kuwaitis had imagined that the family would return from exile converted to democracy and open government. It was debatable how many actually wanted these things. A genuine democracy, extending the franchise to long-term residents, would mean a reduction in the power and privileges that only Kuwaitis had previously enjoyed. Even the most progressive of the dissidents was not keen on that. As for the rest, a newspaper poll suggested that opinion was evenly divided on whether or not it was a good idea to give Kuwaiti women the vote.

The image of Kuwait as a business corporation was an old one, but it fitted the facts. What the shareholders wanted was not workers' control, but a bigger say in the management and a bigger share of the dividends. This, it seemed, was a more powerful source of discontent than concern about human rights or hankerings after democracy for its own sake.

These considerations seemed to outweigh the new political forces that had been created by the fact of occupation and war. In other circumstances it might be expected that a returning government-in-exile might face a considerable challenge from those who'd stayed behind, especially from leaders of the resistance. The resistance appeared to have been much more formidable than had first been thought. In some areas of the city like Rumaithia, armed opposition to the invaders had carried on for two months after the occupation. Local committees organised food distribution and medical care as well as gathering intelligence and sending it out of the country. All the major factions in Kuwaiti society were involved in this: radicals, merchants, fundamentalists, Shias, even a small group representing the al Sabahs. The cohesiveness of the network was finally damaged, however, when the Iraqis raided a meeting at which all the elements had come together to form a unified command structure.

That meeting had taken place on 22 October at a house in the Nuzha district. Among those present were two senior Kuwaiti army officers and a police chief. The Iraqi raid was apparently a coincidence, a routine house search. They arrested one of the army officers, the police chief and seven other leaders. The rest escaped but the damage had been done.

One of the most impressive activities of the resistance was the creation of the Kuwaiti Society for the Relief of War Victims, which succoured PoWs before and after the war, keeping tabs on who had been taken away and organising visits. This organisation was treated with suspicion by the government after its return from exile. The head of the Society was told that as it was unlicensed, its activities were technically illegal.

It is easy to see why the thought of resistance structures

carrying over into post-Liberation life – even avowedly non-political ones like the society – should have made the al Sabahs uncomfortable. Even more disturbing was the idea of a resistance hero emerging. The al Sabahs had none to offer, apart from poor Sheikh Fahd, whose ill-timed night on the town had coincided with the Iraqi invasion and proved fatal. Fortunately for the government, the person with the best resistance credentials, General Mohammed al Bedr, the army chief who escaped when the Iraqis raided the resistance leaders' meeting, had declined to capitalise on his status and although close to the opposition groups, had not publicly attached himself to them.

The government was adamant that there was to be no friction between those who left and those who stayed, though the distinction was clearly going to matter in the post-Liberation shake-out. Some of those who stayed behind claimed there was a subtle campaign afoot to denigrate their number. 'The suggestion is that if you stayed, you did so to protect your property,' said a Kuwaiti journalist.

At the end of July 1991, I returned to Kuwait to cover the anniversary of the invasion. The event was being approached by the al Sabahs with a sort of wincing resignation. How do you commemorate a disaster? They had wisely plumped for the anodyne. There was an exhibition of children's paintings, a medium beloved by Arab propagandists from Baghdad to Beirut. There was a three-day symposium in which academics, theologians and journalists were to tackle such cotton-wool themes as 'the effect of the invasion on future Arabic relationships' and 'the rôle of the media in confronting the tyrannical Iraqi invasion.' Nowhere in the programme was there any discussion of the lessons of the invasion for contemporary Kuwaiti society.

If the Gulf War were a morality story, the inhabitants of Kuwait would have returned home resolved to be nicer all round. The rulers would be more democratic, the ruled less lazy. If the Gulf War were a morality story, Saddam Hussein

171

would have been overthrown, his system destroyed and his people liberated. If the Gulf War were a morality story, the new order spoken of by President Bush would have set about correcting all the historical mistakes of arrogant, greedy colonialism that had ensured the political instability of the region.

None of these things happened. The claim of a clear moral purpose made by the West after its intervention proved to be disingenuous. The campaign was fought under a banner of democracy, yet the old firm were back in power as grasping and selfish as ever. It was fought in the name of human rights, yet the first act of the victims of the original injustice was to persecute the Palestinians and the Bedoon. The fight was above all against tyranny, yet the tyrant was still in power. Not merely in power, but also allowed to exercise it in wholesale killing of those who with American encouragement had risen up against him.

On the anniversary of the invasion, I visited the graveyard at Rigga where I had gone on the first day of Liberation. I remembered the scorched corpses of the Iraqis being stuffed into the sand, the neat barrows where the murdered Kuwaitis lay. The graves had headstones now which detailed how their occupants had met their deaths: four youths, killed by the Iraqis when they stormed a house; a man killed by the Iraqis after being betrayed by Palestinians. One imagined future generations pausing by the graves and asking, like the boy in Robert Southey's poem, what it had all been about.

> 'And everybody praised the Duke,
>   Who this great fight did win.'
> 'But what good came of it at last?'
>   Quoth little Peterkin.
> 'Why that I cannot tell,' said he,
> 'But 'twas a famous victory.'